TOYDOGS

TOYDOGS

Harry Glover

Paintings by the author. Photography, Diane Pearce

David & Charles
Newton Abbot   London   North Pomfret (Vt)   Vancouver

ISBN 0 7153 7338 2

Library of Congress Catalog Card Number 77-77610

Set in 11 on 12 point Bembo
and printed in Great Britain
by Biddles Limited, Guildford
for David & Charles (Publishers) Limited
Brunel House   Newton Abbot   Devon

Published in the United States of America
by David & Charles Inc
North Pomfret   Vermont 05053   USA

Published in Canada
by Douglas David & Charles Limited
1875 Welch Street   North Vancouver   BC

CONTENTS

1
IDEAL COMPANIONS

CLOVER

No animal has been adopted and domesticated so completely as the dog. Some cat devotees particularly would deny this and lay claim to the cat as man's most constant and faithful companion, but history has proved, and numbers continue to prove, that pride of place as the most accepted companion of mankind is the dog.

Almost every type and breed of dog can become a companion, whatever its original work happened to be, as has been evidenced in recent years in the toughest breed of all, the husky, which in its native land spends the most bitter of winters out of doors and works like a draught-horse, pulling huge loads over immense distances. A dog that will fight its own kind and even its own family over a bone until one or the other is destroyed unless tethered apart, and one which on the face of it is a most unloving and unloved animal, now is accepted as a companion and welcomes the friendship of mankind in just the same way as almost any other breed of dog.

If dogs of this type can become completely domesticated, how much more so can those breeds of dog that have by tradition and breeding always been house pets and companions as the toydogs have. Bred for generations (even centuries in some cases) to live a life of comfort and leisure, sharing the house, the food and even the bed of his master or mistress, toydogs are the supreme companion.

Those who are sensitive to environment, and to domestic environment in particular claim, and probably quite correctly, that no dwelling-place comes to life until something alive comes into it. Those who live alone and return to an empty house may well feel a sense of deadness. Birds, goldfish, even plants will suffice in a way, but neither a goldfish nor a plant will meet one at the door, and even though a bird is a slight improvement in that it is capable of making a noise which may be interpreted as

a welcoming sound, it cannot express the same degree of joy at a reunion as a dog.

Whilst it is true that heredity has dictated that certain characteristics are peculiar to certain of the toydog breeds, they all have one thing in common – they all love mankind and all enjoy his way of life. Hounds, gundogs and other types that enjoy the warmth of the fireside will show pleasure at being treated from the table (a practice that is deplored but goes on nevertheless) and will welcome every opportunity to spend time with human beings. As a result they are considered to be very much companion dogs even though they have other characteristics associated with the work that they do. As a result there has grown up a sort of mystique about having a working type of dog as a companion. It is considered, or was at one time considered, to be more manly to have a gundog or hound at one's heel or at one's fireside than it was to have say a Pekingese or a Pomeranian. It was something of a cult to wear hairy tweeds, carry a knobbly stick and stamp around with a cocker spaniel or Labrador retriever, even if shooting anything was the last thing one thought of. This resulted in a great upsurge of popularity of certain bigger dogs. Alsatians, golden retrievers and Labradors became a symbol of this type of life. They were large, had the deep-throated bark of the bigger dogs, and represented an activity and a lifestyle which was considered the appropriate thing in a rural situation, which was urban man's interwar years way of expressing his masculinity.

Many attitudes changed as a result of the involvement in two world wars. Civilised man was suddenly thrust into a way of life which at one and the same time dragged him away from everything he had thought of as immutable – his house and garden, his walks in the country and his occasional fishing or hunting trips – and thrust him into a situation in which all he really longed to do was to return to everything that represented all that was best in his old way of living. During wartime there was also a premium on

(*facing page*) Long coat Chihuahua

masculinity so that not only did men dream of their former life-style, but it was heightened by images of such things as guns and dogs, walks through the countryside and afterwards sitting smoking a pipe in front of a roaring fire with a dog panting contentedly at their feet.

Unfortunately the toydogs had nothing of this mystique about them. They were ladies' dogs, soft effeminate things that could do nothing. They yapped instead of barked, would run at the sight of a rabbit (but in the wrong direction), and would be an object of scorn if they pranced into the local at one's heels. After a while, however, it was realised that none of this was true. Certainly they yapped, but a yap is as good as a throaty bark to waken a household, and a poodle would deter an intruder every bit as well as would a Pyrenean mountain dog. When it came to walks in the country a toydog was as good a companion as any other. In fact it had added advantages – as this was the age of the motorcar, a small dog could fit into a small car more easily.

The mess and damp deposited on the upholstery of a modern car by a Yorkshire terrier, was not nearly as destructive as it was when it was left there by an Irish water spaniel, and many people learned to their astonishment that instead of running in the opposite direction, a Pekingese would chase a rabbit with the best of them and with more enthusiasm and energy than most.

In the period immediately after World War II when things were still very martial and when the remaining army units liked to display their prowess at our agricultural shows by rushing into the arena and letting fly a few rounds of blanks, the dogs that broke loose from their benches and chains were not the toydogs, who took it all with a certain phlegm, but the larger dogs, and the gundogs. These were often seen disappearing in all directions after the first blast. In fact the toydogs as a group are very sporting little animals, full of fun, enjoying life to the full and making the most of every opportunity to display their tremendous activity and agility. Being, as they are, large dogs wrapped up in small packages, they have all the muscularity and strength of a large dog, but less weight to move and quicker reactions, resulting in more activity per pound than the larger breeds.

(*facing page*) Pekingese

2 ATTRIBUTES OF TOYDOGS

We have always interested and amused ourselves by changing, to suit our own ends and purposes, those creatures with which nature presents us. Shape, texture, colour and size have all been altered, and particularly size so that animals have been miniaturised for as long as they have been accepted into our home and company. In no species has this been more marked than in the canine race. Beginning with common ancestors, all of which looked very much alike, knowledgeable selective breeding has down the centuries brought about so many changes of size that the difference between say the **Great Dane and the Chihuahua** make them appear so unlike that they do not look as though they belong to the same breed. In making these changes breeders have made the development of smaller and smaller examples one of their favourite pursuits, seemingly to display to the world their skill in much the same way that the eighteenth-century miniature painters produced ever-smaller portraits or the Italian jewellers and silversmiths created masterpieces of the metalworkers' skill in the smallest possible compass.

The result of this interest in creating smaller creatures in the world of dogs has led to a collection of small animals fashioned purely for the pleasure that they give their owners. They do not as a rule do any work; they do not hunt, guard or pull loads, although they will in fact do all these things for fun if called upon to do so. They have been created for pleasure, to grace a household, a carriage, milady's knee, or even more prosaically, a motorcar, and to be pampered and petted instead of being kept out in kennels as gundogs and hounds are, waiting for an opportunity to show how well they can work. For want of a better term and largely because of their size – or rather their lack of it – they have earned the title of toydogs. The word covers, in different countries, a group of breeds of dog that vary slightly, but basically they all

(facing page) Yorkshire terrier

CLOVER

have one thing in common: they are small.

The history of the association between man and dog goes back into the shadowy past long before records were kept, to a time when the connection was almost certainly tenuous and brought about by the natural scavenging habits of the canine race. At that time dogs were almost certainly purely guards, performing that function more by chance than design, simply being around the tribe and giving warning of the approach of anything that appeared strange or dangerous. It would not be until very much later that dogs were trained to work and later still that they were accepted as companions. Taking a fully grown timber-wolf into the house, petting it and allowing it to sit on one's knee, appears to present certain difficulties and it is probable that it would be the weaklings and the smaller specimens that would, in the first instance, enjoy these privileges.

The reasons for people enjoying the company of dogs are complex, but it is almost certain that the mothering instinct plays a large part, and it may be natural for children and the ladies of the household to prefer to extend this sort of feeling towards something diminutive. So the first criterion of the toydog is that it must essentially be small, it must be possible for it to be picked up, to share a chair, a settee or even a bed, to be carried around as a doll or some other form of plaything is carried. There is a practical limit to the size of animal that can conveniently be carried, and this has led to an animal with a maximum weight – in the case of two of the breeds of toydogs, of 18 lb (8·2 kg).

It is then essential that these small dogs should be temperamentally suited to living in very close proximity to people, enjoying their company, and behaving in such a way that their company in turn is enjoyed by those who own them. This entails a cheerful disposition and an ability to amuse. Most people appreciate an animal that joins in when wanted but does not obtrude when not, one that enjoys being fussed when its owner is in the mood for petting it, yet intelligent and sensitive enough to understand when it is better to retire to its own corner and stay quietly out of trouble.

This need for the company of animals has developed over centuries. Work has kept the men of the house away for long periods, wars for even longer, and the rest of the family, whilst company for one another, have needed the additional companionship of animals around the house. Traditionally the worker's or the farmer's wife took to having a cat to keep her company when the man has been away from home for the major part of the day, but cats are independent creatures and tend not to stay at home at the times when their company is most needed. The result was the development of the small dog as company for the lady of the house.

Another important quality that a toydog must have is that in some way it must have a physically attractive appearance, not necessarily the grace and traditional beauty of form of some of the larger breeds of dogs such as the greyhound and the deerhound, but either a beauty of colour, of coat, or a quaintness of outline or detail which in some way or another makes it appealing. It could be the sheer grace of the Italian greyhound, the silky coat of the Yorkshire terrier, or even the quaint distorted short-nosed appearance of the pug. Whatever it is, a toydog must have something in its appearance that makes it visually pleasing. Above all else it must not be an ordinary-looking dog, it must have the air of quality, of aristocracy even, the quality that a silver teapot has and a brown earthenware one does not.

It is essential that a toydog should have the ability to amuse – not by performing tricks, as this is the province of the trained poodle of circus and stage, but by playing the games which are natural to it. If a large dog such as a bullmastiff tries to catch its tail and in doing so falls over, it is grotesque and a cumbersome

(*facing page*) Early type of toy spaniels

performance and as such can be embarrassing to watch. The same act performed by a pug at several times the speed, with the quickness of recovery from awkward situations that the smaller dog has, becomes a most entertaining spectacle. It is like watching the larger dogs earlier performance through the wrong end of a telescope and having it speeded up conveying an almost dreamlike quality of seeing something that is not really taking place. When a large dog picks up something and shakes it, the movement of the head can be watched from side to side. When the same thing is done by a Yorkshire terrier, the whole head disappears in a blur and the impression is of something almost magical taking place.

The same thing happens with cats. The mature cat does not indulge in play so often as does a kitten; the former is too slow and has in any case begun to relate the chasing of a ball of wool to the more sanguinary business of catching something living to eat. The kitten, in contrast, plays for the sake of play and as a result performs the most unlikely antics purely and simply for the joy of movement, with the result that the positions in which it finds itself and the incredible recoveries that it makes from those positions provide enjoyable entertainment. The kitten is a miniature cat, in the same way that a toydog is a miniature dog, and its size combined with its speed makes for a kaleidoscopic performance for something that we enjoy because we do not quite understand it.

The other quality that toydogs have which is denied to many other breeds is the assurance, the sense of their own importance, the feeling that in every small dog there is a big dog trying to get out. Nothing is more self-important than a Pekingese when it is off on business of its own, whether it is to make sure that the dried-up bone that it attempted yesterday to bury in the rosebed is still there, or whether it is still making sure that the cat next door is not behind the summerhouse. He, or it could be she as the bitches are equally good at it, walks with a pompous nose-in-the-air

(*facing page*) Playful Pomeranians from the painting by Maud Earl

attitude, scorning the very grass on which his proud feet are forced to tread. Many of the other breeds of dog fail to have this quality. A cocker spaniel will fawn – something that hardly any of the toydogs will do – a wire fox-terrier will condescend to have its ears rubbed and a whippet will make a cautious approach for attention, but a toydog will meet a human being on level terms, being neither over-effusive nor reserved, neither too boisterous nor too cautious. A toydog knows that it is wanted for its own sake and will act as an equal, never as a second-class citizen.

Most, but not all, of the toy breeds have this self-important quality. The members of the species have ancestors divided among the other groups of dogs almost equally: the Italian greyhound is basically a member of the hound group, the Yorkshire terrier is still a terrier and the King Charles spaniel a spaniel, but somehow in becoming smaller they have had to compensate, with the result that their more positive qualities have overcome the others. In common with other animals that have enjoyed the company of people for many generations, even centuries, the intelligence of toydogs has developed as their physical attributes have shrunk. Spending almost all their life in close contact with human beings, they attain an almost quasi-human ability to comprehend.

Those who are familiar with dogs that have been trained to do obedience work, or who have seen dogs performing in the obedience ring at a show, will know that the ability to carry out orders comes from a constant reiteration of the same command given with the same intonation over a long period of training, so that the dog knows what its owner wants it to do from the way a command sounds rather than from the word itself. The toydog, through close contact with the same human being over a number of years, becomes aware of what certain words mean from the sound of them, with the result that one hears frequently the claim 'He knows just what I say.' This familiarity with sounds made by human beings leads to perception which is denied dogs that have not the same close contact, with the result that the toydogs have gained the reputation of an acute intelligence and a decided awareness. Through this association they have also developed a certain contempt for the human race, but this fact adds rather than detracts from their appeal.

As the result of this close contact with us, most toydogs are eminently trainable. They enjoy their closeness, are anxious to please, and are as delighted at something successfully understood and achieved as an intelligent child would be. Oddly enough, few toydogs have made their mark in the obedience show ring, and with one or two quite notable exceptions they do not take kindly to the type of work involved. It is possible that there can be such a thing as too much intelligence. If a dog cannot see the sense of doing a certain thing, it may do it, but only with reluctance. Toydogs are hardly ever reluctant, so it could well be that on the whole they understand too well, and prefer not to perform.

Toydogs have a sense of humour – they will enjoy the same practical joke over and over again. They don't in fact laugh any more than other breeds of dog – and dogs do laugh – but they succeed in conveying the fact that they are enjoying themselves without actually grinning. Her Imperial Majesty Dowager Empress of the Flowery Land of Confucius put it well when she said of the Pekingese:

Let it be taught to refrain from gadding about; let it comport itself with the dignity of a duchess. Let it be lively that it may afford entertainment by its gambols; let it be wary that it may not involve itself in danger; let it be sociable in its habits that it may live in amity with the other beasts, fishes or birds that find protection in the Imperial Palace.

If the image conveyed is that of a lively, intelligent, companionable and entertaining dog then it is correct, because that is what almost all the toydogs are.

Chinese crested

3
COMPANION DOGS

The breeds of dog that go to make up the group that we now call the toydogs in some cases started life as members of the other family groups. They were either basically spaniels, as the King Charles spaniel, or terriers, as the English toy terriers, and have evolved by a process of miniaturisation from larger breeds. Some of them, and the Pekingese is probably a good example, have existed as tiny dogs for as long as we have known of them, and it would now be impossible to trace their development from anything else; to attempt to do so would result only in surmise.

Pekingese

Accepted by many as the typical toydog, the Pekingese is a very ancient breed whose association with man goes back many centuries. They are one of the most popular breeds in the group and one with considerable appeal. In numbers of registration they cannot quite compete with the Yorkshire terriers, but there are very many of them in the competition rings. The Pekingese is another oriental breed of dog, the royal dogs of China, known sometimes as lion dogs, and their history goes back to at least the Tang dynasty. The first importation of the breed into Britain took place in 1860 when Admiral Lord John was present at the overrunning of the Summer Palace, during which the court fled to the interior leaving five of the royal dogs in the garden. These five were brought back to Britain, Lord John and another officer retaining two each and the fifth being presented to Queen Victoria by General Dunne. The two that spent the rest of their days at Goodwood were the ancestors of many of the Pekingese that were eventually bred in this country. It is interesting that in the early days of the breed it was not difficult to import Peking spaniels from China, but virtually impossible to acquire those

bred in the imperial palace, as they were strictly guarded and theft of them was punishable by death.

From the Goodwood pair the Duchess of Richmond gave away dogs from time to time to such people as the Dowager Lady Wharncliffe and Lady Dorothy Neville, a move which kept the breed on the increase and ensured their continued prosperity. Just before the turn of the century another Pekingese, said to have been another true palace dog, is believed to have been smuggled out of the country by a Mr Douglas Murray who hid him in a box of hay inside a crate of Japanese deer. This dog became Ah Cum, famous in his day. He crossed with some of the Goodwood strain and produced some of the most famous of the breed.

When discussing the history of the Pekingese one talks in terms of dynasties rather than centuries, and so close has their connection been with the court that reigns rather than eras are used in compiling the legends, myths and stories that are told and retold about them. The result somehow shows in the dogs themselves. They have an aloofness and an independence of character that few other breeds have. One could easily be excused for thinking of the 'inscrutable orient', and when they play it is often in a condescending manner which implies that while they are prepared to amuse the humans present, they do it because it is their duty rather than with the wild abandon of many other breeds.

Pekingese are above all else fearless and sporting, which is undoubtedly part of their appeal. They are alert guards and can be quite fierce, even amusingly so for so small a dog, and at one time they were trained to fight. It has been the habit to regard the Pekingese as silly little pampered pets suitable only for the ladies of the household to fuss over, and completely unsuitable as a man's dog. Those who have owned them know them for the vital, strong-opinionated little dogs that they are, every bit as suitable for a long country walk involving a swim and a chase after a rabbit as they are for a tasselled velvet cushion in a centrally

(*facing page*) Griffon

heated boudoir. Much of what has been written in the past about toydogs is myth and legend, and many tales that have been based on fact have themselves over the years achieved the status of a legend very quickly. There is something about the toydogs that promotes stories to be told about them.

It is true that many other breeds of dog have the same effect, the legendary deerhound of Sir Walter Scott, the Hospice of St Bernard and its great dogs, and the Celtic mythological hound of King Arawn, King of the Underworld are examples; but somehow, as a group, toydogs have drawn stories to them as steel to a magnet. It is probably their diminutive size, for there are many legends about other miniatures; elves, fairies, leprechauns and so on. There are probably more tales about Pekingese than about any other dogs. Their whole existence is shrouded in legend – even their very origin. The anecdote goes that a lion journeying through the depths of the forest met a marmoset with whom he fell in love. Their differing sizes meant that there would be certain difficulties about the union, so the lion approached the Lord Buddha, who happened to be around, and prayed to him to make him small enough to find favour with his lady. This the Lord Buddha agreed to do but only if the king of the beasts agreed to sacrifice his size and strength and become one of the smallest of animals. The lion agreed to this and the Lord Buddha recited a prayer which made the lion shrink in size until it was only the same size as the marmoset that it favoured. The Buddha was so impressed by the fortitude and steadfastness of the lion in undergoing this transfiguration that he allowed him to keep his large heart, his form, and his dignity. The lion and the marmoset enjoyed the relationship that they wished for, and their progeny enjoyed the benefits of the courage and form of the lion and the playfulness of the monkey, becoming in the process the Pekingese.

The confusion that exists in ancient Chinese stories as the result of this sort of anecdote, has resulted in no clear line of demarcation

(*facing page*) Pekingese

between the lion and the dog. Even the lion dog (the royal dog of China) as we know it today becomes involved, and a good deal of the theatrical work that is done with men playing the part of animals on the stage of the Chinese theatre (much as our panto-mime has its two-man horses) results in something that is neither dog nor lion, but a wonderfully dramatised decorative creature that has been depicted in Chinese sculpture and pottery for centuries. These figures are full of symbolism. They wear leads which are often entwined into complicated figures, closely resembling in some instances the complicated letters of the Chinese alphabet. The male stands with his foot on a woven ball which is said to have some connection with the power of lion's milk, the female is depicted with one of her paws on the mouth of a cub, a reference to the fable that lionesses suckled through their paws. Almost everything connected with the Pekingese in the early days is apocryphal, and this tradition is continued to the present day in China when in ceremonial processions a lion, or dog-headed creature, is carried accompanied by someone carrying a large coloured ball which the creature stops to play with from time to time. The figure has become so decorative that it is sometimes difficult to distinguish if it is a dog, a lion or a dragon.

The Dowager Empress Tzu Hsi did much to prevent the con-tinuance of the practice of confining small dogs, and Pekingese in particular, in tiny boxes and giving them drugs to prevent them from growing. She took a great interest in the breed, and en-couraged the breeding of small Pekingese by natural selective-breeding methods. She it was who wrote:

> Let its colour be that of the lion – a golden sable,
> To be carried in the sleeve of a yellow robe,
> Or the colour of a red bear, or a black or a white bear,
> Or striped like a dragon, so that there may be dogs,
> Appropriate to each of the Imperial Robes.

The idea of having poodles dyed to match the colour of my lady's outfit, which was in vogue some years ago in America, was not nearly as new as many might have thought at the time. The Chinese, who have been the originators of so much that is aesthetic as well as destructive, were thinking along the same lines centuries before.

Each Pekingese is very much an individual, differing from its fellows in many respects. Unlike breeds with the same colour pattern, they vary greatly in colour, coat and character, so that even members of the same closely related family are easily distin-guished one from the other. They have a wonderfully responsive temperament in spite of their inbred independence, enjoying human company and demanding to be played with in a somewhat similar way to a kitten. They have their favourite toys, traditionally a ball, and they will seek and find like a retriever, displaying intelligence of a high order. Their favourite trick is probably sitting up, something that they do quite naturally. As puppies they dance around on their hindlegs, but as they get older this develops into a natural sitting posture which they use, not for begging purposes, but just to join in the company of their human companions. Pekingese have been companions for so long that they seem to have forgotten that they are dogs, and look upon themselves as small human beings.

Above all else, Pekingese are proud dogs. Their long heritage, their centuries of association with people and the fact that at all times they have been treated in a very special way, has undoubtedly led them to believe that they have exceptional rights. Once someone takes a Pekingese into their household, they could themselves be taken over by the dog. The dog may dominate, making demands just as a child or even another adult will, and in a short while the whole household could revolve around the Pekingese. One rarely hears of Pekingese being maltreated – it is as though no one dared to take such liberties. A large dog sometimes needs to be mastered, and this leads to beatings that may eventually turn to vicious ill-treatment. A Pekingese has the pride of a large dog, but the sort of pride that in so small an animal is found amusing rather than challenging by humans.

The diminutive size of the Pekingese will not deter it from hunting. They are natural explorers and will follow a scent with concentration, but when the exercise is over they will relax in the most human manner, sighing like tired old men and settling down into the deepest sleep, often in somewhat peculiar positions, but with an air of comfort that is in itself a relaxation to watch. They will settle down in front of the fire just as any dog will and will play the part of the returning warrior every bit as much as will the biggest and strongest gundog or running hound; and the Pekingese will do it with the advantage of taking up considerably less space and needing a good deal less food and water.

At one time the eunuchs of the imperial palaces of China amused themselves by arranging dog fights between the ordinary Pekingese that were commonplace in the country as distinct from the palace dogs which were very special animals. History has it that these fights were very ferocious and were considered major sporting events. The Pekingese at that time would clearly need to be anatomically somewhat different from the present-day specimens, but the temperament remains the same: although Pekingese dogs will not generally seek a fight, they will enjoy one to the full if it does develop. This dispels the often-held opinion that they are soft little dogs fit only to sit on someone's knee. They have a remarkable degree of independence, and yet at the same time they are wonderful companions. They do not attach themselves to one person quite so firmly as some of the other breeds, having instead a highly developed territorial instinct, guarding a house and its garden and defending it fiercely against any intruder. They have great charm of manner, being dogs with more personality than most.

As a breed they are so important, and as dogs they have such individual characteristics, that they earn for themselves a separate place in any book on toydogs. From the point of view of appearance, if they had to be grouped in any family at all it would have to be the spaniel family: they share something of the proportions and the pendant ears of that group. Indeed there is a certain resemblance between the Pekingese and the Tibetan spaniel which is geographically a fairly near neighbour, is around the same size and has at times even been confused with the Pekingese, even though it does not belong to the toydog group at all.

Pug

Most of the short-nosed toydogs with curly tails came from the Far East, and the pug is no exception. Many of the animals depicted in ancient pottery and carving have the short, broad, wrinkled face of the pug. Even the lion carvings decorating Chinese temples look more like pugs than lions. At one time it was thought that the pug came from Holland, which in fact some of them probably did, but this was an example of accepting obvious facts without digging deeper. They were even known at one time as Dutch pugs. It is more than likely that pugs were introduced to Holland by the traders of the Dutch East Indian Trading Company who brought them from China. They were very popular in Holland at the end of the eighteenth century, and a certain amount of indiscriminate breeding took place.

Pugs have an entirely different character from the Pekingese, although they too are very much the lap dog despite the fact that they tend to prefer to occupy the most comfortable chair or settee rather than a lap. In a very small compass they are heavy little creatures, and although they must be classified as a companion dog purely and simply they still have a good deal of independence of character. Whilst they love to spend their time with the people of their choice, they are quite happy in the company of one another, and even on their own, and will depart on expeditions that have nothing whatsoever to do with the family or even the house.

They endear themselves to their owners in many different ways. Some people like them because they have the settled characteristics of old people, tending to sit in a chair and ruminate. Some enjoy their endless *joie de vivre*, they are rarely miserable or out of sorts, enjoying a romp of their own choosing and designed by them-

selves, the quiet sort of rolling and pushing romp to which their anatomy is best fitted. Some owners like them because of the strange noises that they make. Being an excessively short-nosed breed, they tend to snort and rumble like ancient crones or old men, and they can often be heard in the quiet of the household approaching a room with sounds which resemble, to the uninitiated, those of a miniscule and strange wild beast.

They are without doubt aldermanic. Their tendency to obesity, their heavyweight, deeply-folded, appealing expression and the wheezy 'old-man' noises they make leaves one with the feeling that when encountering a pug one is being interviewed by a local council official for a position in the town's waterworks. They are not as playful as many of their fellows in the toydog group: they are not built for it. While they enjoy a romp among themselves, they do so with a certain ponderousness and not with the same gay abandon that some of the other breeds display.

The staunchest advocate of the breed would hardly claim that they are sporting dogs. They are quite fearless and self-willed, but their hunting instinct is not as highly developed as some of the other breeds. Indoors they like their comfort, demanding the most comfortable chair and always enjoying their food. As mentioned above, they have a tendency to putting on weight, which needs to be carefully controlled as their physical characteristics are not of the best for this sort of indulgence – but they have a way of appealing for food that makes them difficult to resist. They enjoy being out of doors, and of all the dogs that one sees being walked in the parks of the large cities, the pug appears the most popular. In fact if there is any scene that is more typical of a park than any other it is 'lady with pug'.

Pugs are quite effusive in their approach to people, and even complete strangers, once they have been introduced and accepted, are greeted like long-lost friends. The dogs' shape, and their tightly curled tail, do not lend themselves to the same joyous

(*facing page*) Pug

display that some other breeds give, but the way in which they wriggle their whole body and manage to manipulate their tail makes it quite clear that they are happy to meet people. Most judges of dogs find that when they approach a pug on the table at a show, they are in for a greeting that will include a good deal of wriggling and almost certainly a licked welcome as well. They are most enjoyable dogs to own because they themselves enjoy being owned. As entertainers they do not reach the heights of some other breeds. They do not perform tricks that demand any degree of anatomical dexterity and they have too much will of their own to be trained to perform easily, either tricks at home or obedience for competition, but their almost-human behaviour and manner is every bit as entertaining.

These little dogs have always gained the hearts of those people fortunate enough to own them, and oddly enough Dr John Caius, author of *Treatise on English Dogs* (1576) referred to one of the toy breeds as 'A pleasant playfellow. A pretty Worme', a term of endearment that must have referred to their habits rather than their appearance. In the early nineteenth century it was the habit to write tributes to pets in the form of epitaphs, and in the year 1818 there appeared in the *Sporting Magazine* for April the following tribute to Fanny, the favourite pug of Her Royal Highness the Duchess of York, written by Mr Upton:

> Reader tread lightly o'er this mound of earth,
> Nor give, while here, too loose a rein to mirth.
> Beneath this grass, the once gay Fanny lies;
> Her breath now stopp'd for ever closed her eyes.
> 'Tis strange perhaps, yet not more strange than true,
> Fanny was lov'd by man and woman too!
> Nay, even babes would leave their mother's arms,
> To hug, embrace, and gaze on Fanny's charms!
> Yet Fan had faults, and faults, as will appear,
> She never gave to misery a tear:—

> Misfortune, sorrows, or the prisoner's groan,
> Ne'er drew a sigh, nor touched her heart of stone!
> Yet was her nature soft, as soft can be,
> No mortal breath'd more innocent than she.
> Her harmless tongue ne'er utter'd slander's sting;
> The gentle Fanny hurt no living thing:
> Courteous, well bred, engaging and polite;
> The same creature morning, noon and night:
> Not that she did so, by religion taught,
> Fanny ne'er gave religion e'en a thought.
> As nature prompted, she obey'd her will –
> From first to last, the gentle Fanny still!
> Alike the favourite of both poor and rich,
> She live'd and died, a little-little bitch.

Pugs are lovable creatures, and are easily trained. One of the regular spectacles at one of the most highly organised dog shows in the world, The Pal International Show in Sydney, Australia, is a parade in costume of dogs and owners. An almost annual winner at this parade is a lady who has trained her pugs to ride in a rickshaw. She dresses herself in full colourful Chinese costume, and the pugs in the most gorgeous oriental jackets. They sit philosophically in the rickshaw surrounded by candles in lanterns, and all the glitter and colour of the East, whilst their proud owner lopes around the arena with them to the noisy acclaim of the audience. They appear to enjoy it every bit as much as the crowd. They even seem to be laughing, probably as much entertained by the crowd as the crowd is by them. They are exceptionally well-trained and despite the movement and quite severe jolting of their vehicle they do not move at all, sitting impassively regal as if to prove their association with the ancient courts of the East.

(*facing page*) Griffon

Griffon

It sometimes happens that two breeds of dog, or rather two varieties, which have a good deal in common but at the same time features which make them very different, are lumped together for the sake of convenience and shown as the same breed. It happened with the Chihuahuas for a long time, and still does with the Griffon. There are two distinct types of griffon: the Bruxellois, which is the rough-coated variety, and the Brabançon, which has a smooth coat. It seems hard on the Brabançon that it has to lose its identity and be catalogued by the Kennel Club as Griffon Bruxellois.

Like so many breeds of dog with a recent history, the origin of the griffon is difficult to trace. The griffons of one sort or another were fairly common in France, but they bear little resemblance to the one that we know, except for the quality of coat. They were large hunting dogs, varying from the basset to the gundog and the spaniel type, and it is hardly likely that any of them could have resulted in the tiny griffon that we know today. It is suggested that they originated in Belgium where they were primarily a guard dog, and that pugs, terriers and toy spaniels all had a hand in their ancestry. Whatever happened, the result is one of the most attractive of all toydogs, with its quaint expression, large head and eyes and somewhat strange outline. Although their origins are so obscure, almost all the dogs that stemmed from France and Belgium with the word 'griffon' tacked on to their name were dogs that were used for sport, and it is probable that whilst the word implies a rough coat it could well be a term that was particularly used among the sporting fraternity. Certainly these little dogs were very much more than just pets, and in the same way that working men used all sorts of rough terriers for the sport of ratting, so the coachmen of Brussels used these little rough-coated dogs for the same amusement. They still love sport of any sort and, given the opportunity, will show all the terrier interest in rats and mice.

Griffons are something of a dual-personality dog, at times being so supercilious that it is painful, and at others indulging in the most common pastimes and becoming fussy and devoted. They have the terrier's independence of disposition, and with their minds bent on something that is very much their concern they will ignore their closest friend. In addition they are flexible – they will thoroughly enjoy a life in the town, living indoors and appreciating the warmth and comfort of domestic surroundings, but they are equally at home in the country, roughing it, ratting around and spending a good deal of time out of doors. So it is possible that if someone is looking for the perfect all-round little toydog that will take anything that comes along in the best possible spirit and in the best of health, a griffon is the right breed of dog for them.

Griffons are most engaging little dogs. They retain a good deal of the terrier quality of their ancestors, being bred originally as a ratting dog for the ordinary citizen rather than a companion to grace the houses of the affluent, with the result that they still have something of the quality that is known as 'varminty'. In appearance they are the gamin of the toydog world, and something of this seems to come through into their character. They are charming, but in the same way in which an earthy farmer has charm, rather than the cultivated charm of the actor. As was once said of a certain griffon: 'if that dog wore a hat it would be a cloth cap, and he would wear it on the side of his head'. These dogs are intelligent, responsive and sensitive, and as a result make excellent show dogs, appearing to know just what is going on in the ring, and seeming to appreciate that their behaviour and manner is an important part of what is happening. Historically they are a fairly new breed, and something of the fresh brashness of this fact seems to show. Those who have owned a griffon say that they do not want any other breed of dog, as they find them ideal companions, good guards and very intelligent. They have an independence of manner and a nonchalant attitude that endears them to many people, and whilst their appearance is more a matter of charm of character shining out than beauty as it is usually understood, many people find this very fact attractive.

Compared with other toy breeds perhaps they lack the grace and obvious signs of aristocratic breeding, to which they lay no claim. They are very much the dogs' dog, the ordinary man's toydog, and while there exists some evidence in early paintings that a dog very much like the griffon was kept in some of the larger houses, they still look very much more at home in less pretentious surroundings. From the first registration in America in 1903, careful selection has created a dog which is now accepted throughout the world as one of the classics of the toydog world, tiny, gay, typifying the idea of a small dog full of its own importance. The griffon will stand up to the biggest dog it meets and is a great favourite, not only as a pet, but in the highly competitive world of the show ring.

Chihuahua

The Chihuahua is essentially an American dog, and its growth in popularity in that country between 1923, when the breed club was formed, and 1955, a mere thirty years or so, was phenomenal, the registrations at that time running at more than 2,000 each month. Great Britain was slow in adopting the dog, and it was not until after World War II that it started to become popular. For a while the two different coats were shown together, but in recent years they were divided and now the two rival one another for attention of serious breeders and exhibitors. Their minute size, their tremendous sense of their own importance and the intelligence that they display endear them to the showgoing public more than almost any of the other toydogs. In addition they are one of the toydogs that take readily to obedience training, and to see them carrying out the tests with miniaturised equipment is a revelation to those who do not know the breed well and always causes a sensation.

The Chihuahua was said to be sacred to the Aztecs, to be descended from an early mute dog of South America, to have started life with the Incas, to have been reared for food. Almost all the stories for its existence as a separate and distinct breed of small dog have been invented and told and retold, until it becomes difficult to differentiate between the possible and the probable. There is a chance that the breed originated in China, certainly the Mexican hairless dog is called the Chinese dog in Mexico, and there is evidence that in the eighteenth century tiny dogs were seen in Mexico that were said to be on their way from China to Europe. The first of the tiny dogs bought by Americans were in fact obtained in Mexico and some of them were purchased by one of the early American dog judges, James Watson, who managed to buy one in 1888 in El Paso. He stated at the time that variety in colour, shape, size and coat was marked. They have been bred

(*above*) Short coat Chihuahua

(*facing page*) Long coat Chihuahua

down in size until they are the smallest dogs in the world, and they have never been used for any sporting purpose. But they are good guard dogs, being very possessive and making collectively as much noise as a pack of hounds although in a rather higher key.

The stories about the breed, mostly legendary, are so many and so varied that one can choose between them being sacrificed or eaten, perhaps even both, but to look upon them as defenceless little beasts would be quite wrong, as they can and do bite quite fiercely when so inclined. Possibly because they have been bred down to size, they tend to be shy when young, nervous of the attention of strangers and with a tendency to look a little scared. This means that as puppies they need encouraging to be more courageous, and to face up to the world with more boldness and spirit unless are to spend their life being scared of people. When they mature, however, they become quite fearless and will tackle anything that they think is approaching too near either themselves or their property. They become very attached to people and places, making themselves very much part of the family and adopting as a very personal place, their own particular quarters, whether it be somewhere in the house or part of the garden. They are lively and somewhat noisy little dogs and they could well be thought to have some relationship with terriers, as their habits of rushing round barking, exploring and digging when the opportunity presents itself have much the same sort of quality as terriers. They have, however, much more the appearance of the spitz breeds with their prick ears and tails over their backs.

It is strange that many of the indigenous dogs of the world look alike, the dingo of Australia, the semi-wild dogs of India and Ceylon, the basenji of Africa and the common smooth chow-like dog of the Far East all have a great deal in common. It could well be that this type represents the culmination of the mixture of all types of common dog. Certainly the Chihuahua has many of the physical characteristics common to these native dogs. It is un-

likely, therefore, that there is anything of the terrier in them, but they are sharp, quite keen to display displeasure with their teeth, have a keen sense of hearing, and express themselves very vocally. When together, in a pack, they set one another off, and if one barks at an intruder, or a suspected intruder, the rest join in until the sound multiplies many times the number of dogs that are actually there.

The smooth-coated ones have little protection from the cold, and so like their comfort. They are real lap dogs, thoroughly enjoying being nursed and fussed. They will settle on someone's knee for hours, curling up and keeping warm, and grumbling at being disturbed. They are affectionate and very much a one-man dog, attaching themselves to one member of the household to the exclusion of others. They are fearless, and like the Pomeranian, cause a great deal of amusement by the way in which they stand up to huge dogs in the show ring, defying them to come any closer on pain of instant death.

Chinese Crested

The Chinese crested dog, a rare breed, is more popular in America than in Britain. They have a history that goes back centuries, and are one of the short list of 'hairless' dogs. But they are not completely hairless, as they carry a tuft of hair as a crest on their head and a small brush on tail and feet. They almost certainly came originally from China and travelled via Africa and possibly South America, where they were confused with the Mexican hairless dog and the *Canis africanus*, the hairless dog of Africa. To many people they look strange, even rather repulsive as their hairless patchy skin has a reptilian look that many people have difficulty in associating with the canine race. If one is prepared to look upon them as an animal rather than just as a dog, however, they have a certain quaint attractive quality that seems to be appealing to more and more people, as the popularity of the breed is increasing.

They have a tremendous attraction for the popular press, and when representatives of the media attend a show the Chinese crested are certain to get more than their fair share of the attention and the publicity. As a show dog they at present lack uniformity of size and boldness of character. When both these characteristics have been attended to by careful selective breeding, as they undoubtedly will, this will be one of the really attractive additions to the toy group.

(*facing page*) Chinese crested

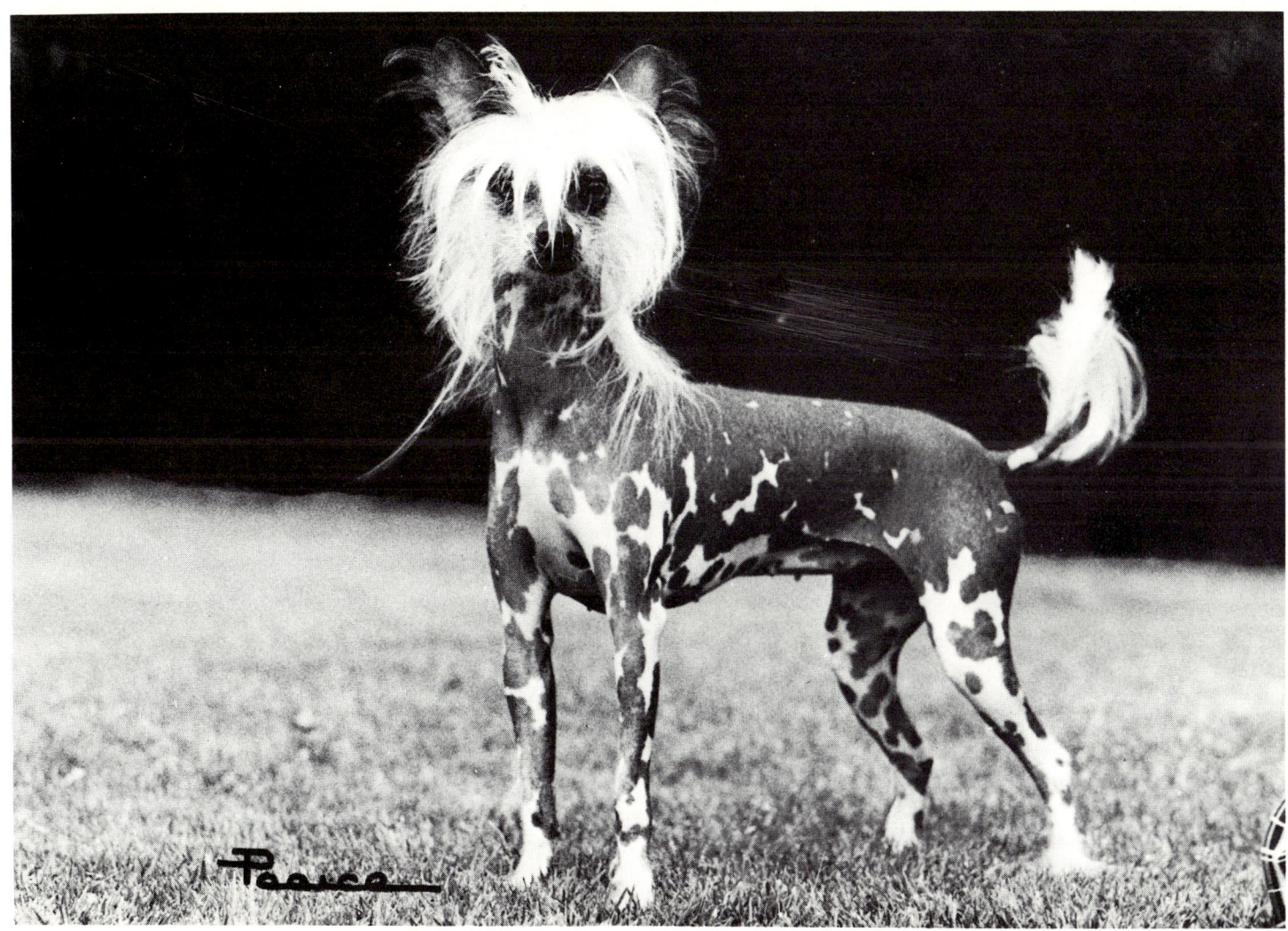

Mexican Hairless

The Mexican hairless proper *is* completely hairless, and was known at one time as the xoloitcuintli. They are similar to Chinese crested dogs, having the same characteristic changes of colour. Vero Shaw, author of *The Illustrated Book of the Dog*, in 1882, mentions the Mexican hairless (although he does not call them such) almost in the same breath as the Chinese crested. At the same time he mentions another oriental dog for which he has no title at all, but which was given to him having come direct from China.

His book contains a fine illustration of what is undoubtedly a shiba, a breed of dog that is enjoying a recent revival of interest in some continental countries. The larger shibas are too large to be considered toydogs, but there is said to be a smaller version, which, if it becomes popular, could well be included in the group. They are of the spitz type once more, with curly tail and pricked ears, and have a fine thick coat with something of the quality of a smooth chow chow. Dogs of this type are rare, although the larger specimens are frequently seen on the waterfront of Hong Kong, probably having been originally adopted by the fishermen travelling between China and Japan.

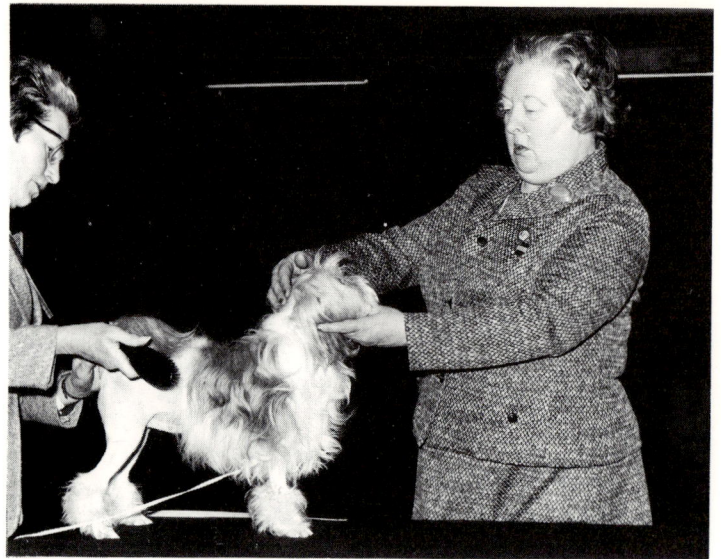
Lowchen

Lowchen

This remarkable little dog is at present enjoying something of a vogue. Known at one time as the little lion dog, they are definitely toydogs and were listed as pet dogs by Robert Leighton in his book of seventy years ago. They are, however, not nearly as small as the toy poodle, a breed that is included among the non-sporting breeds and not among the toydogs at all, but this is just one of the vagaries of the pedigree dog cult. Poodle fanciers do not like them on the whole, as they see in them a very strange-looking poodle, in just the same way that many cocker spaniel advocates do not like the American cocker spaniel. The Lowchen does have something of the look of a poodle, but this is largely because of its coat. The dog is very different around the head. Temperamentally they are delightful little dogs, being most friendly, fairly bold and full of fun. It is one of the general characteristics of all the toydogs that they love people. Their purpose in life is to be companions and, as they were once called, 'comforters'.

Shock Dog

Many centuries ago there existed a little dog called a shock dog, which was probably the ancestor of many of our toydogs. Although not exactly a toydog, the shock dog was small, was not intended to work for its keep, and was typical of the small companion dogs of its time, so it can well be included among these tiny dogs of which stories can be told.

Thomas Carlyle had a shock dog of which he was fond and of which he wrote: 'Poor little Nero, the dog, must have come this winter. The railway guard brought him in one evening late. A little Cuban shock, almost white – a most affectionate, lively little dog, otherwise of small merit, and little or no training ... Poor little animal, so loyal, so loving, so naive and true with what of dim intellect he had.'

Mrs Carlyle clearly did not agree, at least not about the dim intellect, as she wrote of it 'Oh Lord! I forgot to tell you I have got a little dog, and Mr C. has accepted it with amiability. To be sure when he comes down gloomy in the morning or comes in wearied from his walk, the infatuated little beast dances round him on his hind legs, as I ought to do and can't and he feels flattered and surprised by such unwonted capers to his honour and glory.'

There are other toydogs existing in small numbers in relatively remote parts of the world. Mostly they are variations on accepted breeds, but some will eventually be discovered and developed by enthusiasts. In addition there are from time to time attempts made to miniaturise some of the well-known breeds. Some of these fail because the result is often a grotesque example of the larger ancestor. Bull-terriers present a typical case. At present bull-terriers and miniature bull-terriers are accepted breeds, but at one time there was a breed of toy bull-terriers bred down to under 3lb (1·4 kg) in weight. One of the more recent attempts was the miniaturisation of the Afghan hound by crossing it with the whippet, but the effort came to nothing.

Smooth coat Chihuahua

4
TERRIERS

English toy terrier

One particular subgroup of toydogs is that composed of the breeds that owe their origin to the terriers. The Yorkshire terrier and the English toy terrier are typical examples. The miniature pinscher and the Maltese are not quite so clearly associated, and there will be adherents of both breeds who will deny that they are terriers at all. All four, however, have certain characteristics that evidence some earlier terrier connections. They are all somewhat fiery, are exceptionally good guards being very territory-conscious, and have the sharp features and keen expression of the genuine members of the terrier group.

Yorkshire Terrier

Yorkshire terriers lay no claim to antiquity. They do not appear on ancient burial urns, nor are they to be found on cave sides in Egypt. They are a modern breed, produced in Yorkshire, a stronghold of breeders of all forms of livestock from sheep to canaries. Those Yorkshiremen who decided to produce a toy terrier knew exactly what they wanted and set out to manufacture it. They had a good start with the rough black-and-tan terrier and by adding a touch of Skye terrier, a little Maltese and a dash of either dandie dinmont or Clydesdale, they produced one of the great favourites of the toydog group. The rough black and tan gave them their colour, still a very important feature of the breed, and although the black became steely blue as the coat became longer, the tan colour remains all important. The Skye and the Clydesdale gave the long silky coat and helped to convert the black to the blue, and both gave the fire and real terrier quality that this remarkable little dog has retained. The tiny Maltese helped in the process of miniaturisation and added to the length of the coat, and the dandie dinmont was probably the catalyst that completed the transformation. All this is impossible to prove, and even if those who were responsible for the early development were still alive they would deny it all, as early breeders were extremely secretive about their methods. Few experiments in cross-breeding are documented and we just need to take the final result on trust.

The Yorkshire terrier is an out-and-out terrier in spite of the petting and coddling that it gets, and in spite of its effeminate-looking long coat that needs constant attention. It is not just a terrier in name, it behaves like one, with all the temperamental traits of other terriers, and is firmly convinced that it is quite capable of dealing with the biggest vermin that happen along. The fact that they often lose their teeth at an early age does not seem to matter to them at all and they will mumble on a mouse like an old woman mumbling over a piece of toffee, even when they don't have a tooth left. The ones that are used for show do not lose this hunting instinct, and no matter if they are bred for generations from show stock they will still hunt and kill given the opportunity.

One that the author had, bred from generations of show-winning stock, liked nothing better than to be taken on a hunt for mice in the stables where the poultry food was kept. Her record was fourteen mice in ten minutes and her mother, also bred from show specimens, had to be dug out of rat holes on three occasions during her lifetime. It is this natural liveliness that makes it necessary that the coat should be tied up at all times when not actually being shown, and although a Yorkshire terrier looks strange with all its rags in place, if they were not there most of the coat would be rubbed off in play and hunting games even if not in actual hunting. They kill remarkably quickly, and once the small animal is in a Yorkie's mouth it is dead, as one shake is generally enough to dispatch anything small enough for the little dog to get hold of. Unfortunately the spirit of a Yorkshire terrier is indomitable and they will tackle a fully grown rat and get themselves badly bitten in the process, so that it is better to limit their activities to those areas where there are none of the bigger rodents.

My experience with Yorkshire terriers goes back many years. Called Beryl, my first Yorkie was one of the finest watchdogs that it was possible to find. Beryl was only rivalled by a terrier I had very much later, named Wiggy. She too was a remarkably good watchdog, never noisy when it was not needed but a terror when there was anyone about. Her naming was interesting. One of the ways in which the hair of a Yorkshire terrier is kept out of its eyes, is to plait it and tie it up with a short length of ribbon, though this is gilding the lily, as a rubber band will do just as well. It happens that up in the moors fairly near to my family home there is a small village called Wigtwizzle. The appropriateness of

this struck my daughters so forcibly that when we acquired the Yorkie as a tiny puppy, she was registered as Wigtwizzle of Baronslea – Baronslea being my kennels. Wiggy was a tremendous hunter and nothing pleased her more than to be taken out on a mouse hunt. She was a beautiful dog, had a lovely long coat, and would have won many more times than she did, had she not had the unfortunate habit of biting judges. No-one else, no postmen or butcher's boys, just dog judges.

Mr R. Darchambaud, a breeder and judge of Yorkshire terriers for many years, tells of an experience that almost makes one believe that Yorkshire terriers too have that attribute of extra-sensory perception. He sold two dogs to someone who lived about five miles away from his home, a two-year-old bitch and a young dog puppy. The bitch was attached to him, the puppy, sold at eight weeks' old, had obviously not had time to gain the same sort of attachment. The person to whom they were sold is someone that he knows quite well, and who he goes to see from time to time. The puppy has got into the habit of becoming very excited at times, which seem to bear no relation to incidents in his immediate environment. He grows quite agitated, rushes to the door and dances around as though to welcome someone. These demonstrations always occur at exactly the time that Mr Darchambaud starts the engine of his car some five miles away. It is most unlikely that the Yorkshire terrier can hear the car. The dogs have very acute hearing, but five miles' distance is even a bit too far for them and yet, whenever the little dog gets excited in this way, his owner knows for certain that Mr Darchambaud is on his way and gets ready to welcome him.

Like many of the other breeds in the toydog group, Yorkshire terriers love a walk, either on a lead or free in the countryside, preferably the latter, as in the country there is so much to see and hear, and so many new scents. They are virtually tireless, and will take in their stride the exercise that is more normally enjoyed

by much larger dogs, covering many more miles than their human companion as they rush from place to place enjoying the experience of exploration. They are completely fearless and quite incorrigible, appearing to revel in mischief, although not the sort of mischief that is troublesome, just the kind which arises from sheer ebullience. Nothing puts them off, nothing dismays them. They take reverses with complete fortitude and are the greatest of comforts to both children and the elderly.

Yorkshire terriers are both one of our smallest dogs, and one of our most sporting. Attempts have been made to breed them down to a ridiculous size, which many people deplore, and fully grown dogs of under 2 lb (·9 kg) are by no means rare. This is miniaturisation carried to extremes, and really without purpose. Reduction in size to something that fits well into the domestic scene is one thing, but the production of freaks for the sake of creating records is unforgivable.

The number of Yorkshire terriers being bred throughout the world almost certainly exceeds that of any other toy breed. Certainly in Britain they outstrip all their rivals, and the number registered at the Kennel Club annually compares with such popular breeds as Alsatians and Labrador retrievers. They are demanding little dogs, and anyone seeking a quiet life should acquire something else. They are not unnecessarily noisy, but are extremely good guards and very territory conscious, which must involve a certain amount of barking – and their warning is loud, shrill and long. They are most welcoming on the return of a friend, play the role of lap dog with the best of the group, and particularly enjoy a game and a romp based on intelligent use of their hunting instinct. They love a ball game, will retrieve like a gundog, and like hide-and-seek. There is probably no better children's pet than one of these tiny dogs.

(*facing page*) Yorkshire terrier

Miniature Pinscher

The miniature pinscher is an ancient breed, although it was almost certainly not in the form that we know today. The small pinscher of earlier days was often the *Affenpinscher* or monkey pinscher, a tiny wire-haired dog; while at the same time there was a smooth-coated version of the German pinscher. Opinions differ a good deal about the origin of this, perhaps the neatest of the toydogs. It has been suggested that it was arrived at by miniaturising the Dobermann pinscher, but the history of this very much bigger dog is well documented and much more recent than the smaller pinschers. It could well be that somewhere along the line there were common ancestors, but it is very unlikely that there is any close relationship. It is true that when looking at a miniature pinscher, particularly a black and tan one, one gets the impression of looking at a Dobermann through the wrong end of a telescope, but Herr Dobermann had a very different dog in mind when in 1870 he started to develop his breed from the Rottweiler and the old German pinscher.

They are very keen and enthusiastic even though they may not quite be the expert hunters that the English toy terriers are. They are typical terrier type watchdogs, however, and make magnificent guards, defending property with the aggression of much larger dogs. They remind one very much of a quote in the *Sportsman's Repository* of 1820 which when mentioning mastiffs says 'perhaps a large Yard Dog should have an attendant of the smaller kind, whence would arise double security, from the courage of the one, and from the alarm given by the barking of the other. Or a cry of a couple or two of Wappits, make an excellent guard, running from place to place, and encouraging each other to give tongue and tattle on the approach of a stranger.' No one seems to know what a Wappit was, apart from a type of small, noisy vermin catcher and home guard, but certainly the miniature pinscher seems to fill the bill as far as temperament goes. Perhaps someone will revive the breed as a toydog. Certainly the name would cause amusement.

Miniature pinschers have a bold outlook on life, and their attitude in the show ring is very much the same as that of the Pomeranians. They are not exactly fearless, as they have a nervous system that causes them to react quickly to strange or loud noises and they will whip round with remarkable celerity if some strident dog yaps behind them or someone suddenly drops something. They do not cower, but they make sure that the more vulnerable part of their anatomy is not facing towards anything that spells danger. They are classy little dogs, sharp and keen in their outlook as well as in their appearance, and for that reason make a most attractive show dog. As pets they are self-possessed and gay, very intelligent and quick to respond, and while they do not have the sentimental attachment to people of some of the other breeds, they are most companionable and enjoy sharing a house with human beings.

(*facing page*) Miniature pinscher

English Toy Terrier

Towards the end of the nineteenth century one of the most popular breeds of terrier, both for work and show, was the black-and-tan terrier, sometimes known mistakenly as the Manchester terrier. At the same time the black-and-tan toy terrier was produced, either by reducing the size of the existing breed by selection or, as is sometimes suggested, by crossing the black and tan with Italian greyhounds. Whatever the method, it resulted in a tiny dog of around 3–5 lb (1·4–2·3 kg) with the appearance of a black and tan, and with terrier temperament. The breed was later known as the miniature black-and-tan terrier and, more recently still, as the English toy terrier (black and tan), a name which is so clumsy that there is every chance that in the future it will be changed yet again.

In spite of their tiny size, with an average weight of 6–8 lb (2·7–3·6 kg), they remain very much a terrier, hunting, digging and, given the chance, killing. Their forebears were bred and trained for rat killing, a sport which is now illegal but which once enjoyed great popularity among the miners and other working men of the north of England. In this, rats were collected and placed in a wooden surround of a certain size (known as the ratpit) and the dog was then introduced, with the object of killing the cornered rats in a given time. The record is probably held by a black and tan terrier called Billy, who killed 100 rats in 6 minutes 35 seconds. The English toy terrier (black and tan) is descended from this sort of dog, and while it is improbable that any of the tiny modern specimens could emulate Billy's feat, there is no doubt at all that many of them would make the attempt if they were given the opportunity.

Like all the sporting terriers, these little dogs are just as friendly as one could wish. They enjoy human companionship, but demand a return of their affection. They like nothing better than to exercise their natural inclination to hunt, but not to quarter the countryside as a spaniel, nor to run the woodlands like a coursing dog – they prefer the farm building or the rubbish-dump every time. Their natural prey is still the rodents, and there is always a chance that if they are taken for a free run anywhere where there may be rats or mice they will eventually finish up scratching around among the debris of an old wall or trying to turn over pieces of timber in a hunt for anything that tries to escape. Their enjoyment of this form of exercise is a pleasure to watch, and their persistence and intentness is every bit as marked as is that of a border terrier at a foxhole or a wire fox-terrier trying to disturb a rabbit.

Some may wonder why the breed is still known as the English toy terrier (black and tan) but this is because they were once known as black-and-tan terriers, and possibly to avoid confusion that might arise from the fact that there is a toy fox-terrier of a very different colour that is enjoying a certain vogue in the USA. The beauty of the breed lies largely in the quality and colours of its coat. In the 'ideal' specimen those parts which are black must be completely jet black, and those which are tan must be a rich deep chestnut. The pattern of the colours is strictly laid down by the Kennel Club and the breed club, even to pencilling on the toes and a tan spot above each eye. The difficulties of keeping a colour pattern exact in breeding is such that standards must be stringent in order to develop a breed that will keep the ideal pattern.

It is a strange fact that fashion decrees that certain breeds of dog shall become in vogue and thus popular, whilst others disappear. At the time that the black-and-tan toy terrier was at its peak, there was also a blue-and-tan toy terrier with a pale greyish blue colour and pale tan markings; but this has unfortunately disappeared – it could well have been very fashionable in this colour-conscious century.

(facing page) English toy terrier

The Australian Silky

The Australian silky terrier, sometimes known as the Sydney silky, is an interesting breed as it became established only fairly recently. Prior to World War II it was virtually unknown outside Australia, but afterwards became really quite popular in the USA, although even now it is not seen in Great Britain. It is very much a terrier and distinguished from the Yorkshire terrier, to which it owes much of its ancestry, by a much shorter coat; in Australia it is included among the toydog group, and if it becomes popular in other countries it would also come under the toy category.

As would be expected from a breed developed in a country where life has for years been very real and very earnest, this little dog, not much larger than a Yorkshire terrier, is full of fun and a real sport. It was almost certainly developed by mixing Yorkshire terrier, Australian terrier and perhaps a dash of Skye terrier, and is the only true toydog to originate in Australasia. It is unlikely that it will ever oust the Yorkshire terrier as one of the most popular of all the toydogs, as it resembles the Yorkie too closely. It often happens that when two breeds of dog look very similar, one suffers at the hands of the other because it looks like a rather poor specimen of the same breed. But in the case of the Tibetan spaniel, which looks so much like a very poor Pekingese to some people that they confuse the two breeds, has by virtue of its own special qualities rapidly achieved a popularity not thought possible twenty years ago. The breeders of Australian silkies have realised that their dog also could well be appreciated for itself, and have written into the standard of the breed several clauses which prevent confusion – size, length of coat and head characteristics – all of which give the breed a very individual appearance.

(*facing page*) Australian silky

Pearce

47

Maltese

Adherents of this breed would probably deny any relationship between these delightful little toydogs and the terrier group at all, in spite of the fact that they have some of the terrier characteristics and were even known at one time as Maltese terriers. They were also known as the Maltese dog, and are undoubtedly one of the most ancient of the lap dogs of the western world. As records are non-existent it is impossible to compare the length of the history of this breed with some of the oriental ones, but the Maltese could well be the most ancient breed of toydog in the world. They appear to have come from the Adriatic island of Melita rather than from Malta, as their name might imply, and were known in their early days as Melitaers. Dr Caius wrote 'the dogges of this kind doth Callimachus call Melitaers of the Iseland Melita, in the sea of Sicily'. Which is all rather confusing as Melita probably refers to Malta anyway. They were a favourite breed in the time of Phidias, and were favourites of the ladies of the court of imperial Rome. Theophrastus wrote: 'When his favourite dies he deposits the remains in a tomb and erects a monument over the grave with the inscription "Offspring of the stock of Malta".' In many of their paintings of the court, the early Italian painters depicted dogs which were undoubtedly Maltese. Nicholas Froment's (c 1425–83) 'Triptych of the Resurrection', in the Uffizi Gallery in Florence, has a delightful Maltese in the bottom corner. Maltese were probably first imported into England during the reign of Henry VIII, and they were certainly regarded as 'meet playfellows for mincing mistresses' in the time of Elizabeth, to whose Dr Caius we owe so much of our early knowledge of dogs.

Wherever they came from, Maltese are one of the most beautiful of all toydogs, with their wealth of snow-white coat falling to the floor in long fringes. They lay no claim to being highly intelligent

(*facing page*) Maltese

49

– they are not, for instance, as bright as some of the other toydogs, but their ancestral background is not the sort that would lead to a great degree of what is normally accepted as intelligence in a dog. Their origin is claimed by many people to be as ancient or even more ancient than any other breed of dog, but they have always apparently been toydogs and are not descended from a race of dogs that were at any time kept for work. They have been pampered for centuries and have no pretensions to any particular ability to perform as some of the other breeds of dog do. They do not herd sheep nor do they collect game, but it would be an interesting experiment to attempt to train one up to obedience class level.

It is quite remarkable how the characteristics of a breed of dog depend to a large extent upon the stock from which it has descended. Centuries of breeding spaniels for work has resulted in the much-vaunted intelligence of the spaniel race. One of the reasons why some people despise toydogs is because they are said to be lacking in intelligence. As a generalisation this is quite untrue, most of the toy breeds are as bright as their counterparts among the larger breeds, some of them even more so. Maltese are probably the toydog equivalent of say the chow chow. Neither has been bred from working stock, and the one is as likely to have as much (or as little) recognisable *savoir-faire* as the other. That is not to say that they are without wit. Like so many of the other breeds of toydogs, they like a game or a bit of sport, and respond to companionship in much the same way as all the larger dogs. They will hunt and thoroughly enjoy a walk in the country, turning out mice from the stubble and the hedgerows, but unfortunately this ruins their long silky white coat and show specimens need to be denied the pleasure. They have always been depicted with long flowing coat, although never perhaps as long as is now the fashion. It has always been the case that mankind has attempted to improve on nature, and given a dog with a long, white, silky coat like the one the Maltese has, he immediately sets out to make it longer, whiter and silkier. Unfortunately in doing this the tendency is to lose sight of the dog and to prevent it from doing the very thing that it often wants to do.

There is a great deal of pleasure in preparing a dog's coat to absolute perfection, and for the show ring this is essential, but as pets Maltese are probably happier with less coat and that not kept in such pristine whiteness – possibly most of it left among the local brambles. Above all else, Maltese are great fun. They have the comic air of the trained entertainer, and while they have not been used a great deal for this purpose, they have a natural tendency to exaggerate everything that they do. Asked to stand still in the show ring, they do so with an expression of satisfaction in attainment; asked to move, they set off down the ring with an air of jauntiness that would be the envy of many an Irishman going courting in his Sunday best. They attempt to create an impression and will often look around as much as to say 'I'm good and I know I'm good.' They are perfect little housedogs, having no fits of ill-temper, fitting unobtrusively into the routine of the household, and having a coat that does not shed all over the furniture. Being so full of fun they are wonderful pets for children, who find them not only small enough to handle but who enjoy brushing and combing them, looking upon them as a doll.

(*facing page*) Maltese

GLOVER

51

5 GUNDOGS

There are one or two breeds of dog in the toy group which owe something of their ancestry to the spaniel type, either the European spaniel originating as the name suggests in Spain, or the oriental spaniel from which presumably the early Spanish ones developed. Again records are either non-existent or very tenuous, and it is now impossible to prove that the small pendant-eared dogs that appear in early Spanish paintings had, or did not have, a relationship with similar animals in China or Tibet. It is strange, however, that this type of dog developed in two areas of very early civilisation, the Far East and the Mediterranean. There were no similar dogs in the American continent or in any area where a highly developed civilisation came later.

Spain is a typical example of a country where among the wealthy, at least, time was divided between field sports, largely hunting, and the comforts of the court. The records of gundogs in Spain go back centuries. The country has always known fine pointers, as well as a good many special hunting breeds of its own, and the spaniel was an early breed, admired for its work in the field and its appearance and temperament in the home. Spaniels were also admired and coveted by the courts of England and small examples of the breed rapidly became favourites as pets and companions.

King Charles spaniels and Cavalier King Charles spaniels are so alike that they can well be thought of as one sort of dog. They do have differences, both in appearance and character, but these are probably minimal. The Cavalier is much the larger and heavier dog, and as a result of not being so easily petted it has a somewhat greater degree of independence of character. Being descendants of the spaniel of one sort or another, they have retained something of the spaniel temperament. They have the merry outlook of the typical spaniel, enjoying life and showing

(*facing page*) Papillon

53

it. Like spaniels proper they are easily offended and have nothing of the terrier's nonchalant attitude.

They have definitely been bred for the sake of their appearance. The original spaniels from which they came would be much larger and coarser creatures. Hard and accustomed to the chase, they would hardly have been in their original state a typical pet dog, being more accustomed to eating rough and living in the stables than a soft indoor life. They are, however, amusing dogs, and their long association with man is nowhere more obvious than in the use of their shape and form in models from the eighteenth-century potteries, a pair of spaniels being almost essential to any scheme of interior decoration for many decades.

The old books divide the land spaniels (they often divided them into land and water spaniels as well) into three groups. The three that they list are 'the Springer, or large Spaniel, the small or Cocker Spaniels and the small, delicate, domestic spaniel, or Comforter'. If the King Charles spaniels and the Cavalier King Charles spaniels have retained this last characteristic, there is little more that we can ask of them.

King Charles Spaniel

The King Charles spaniel is one of the delightful toys that has evolved from the spaniel of early days, known in the time of King Charles II as just 'spaniel' but undoubtedly, from the evidence of contemporary paintings, toy spaniels. Macaulay writes of the king that 'He might be seen before the dew was off the grass in St. James's Park, striding among the trees playing with his "Spaniels".' Dr Caius describes them thus: 'These dogges are little, pretty, proper, and fyne, and sought for to satisfy the delicatenesse of daintie dames and wanton women's wills, in-struments of folly for them to play and dally withall, to trifle away the treasure of time, to withdraw their mindes from their commendable exercises', a wonderful description of just about all the virtues of a toydog.

One of the few qualities not mentioned in this description is that of faithfulness, and this is best described in Ellis's letters recording the execution of Mary, Queen of Scots: 'Then one of the executioners, pulling off her garters, espied her little dogg which was crept under her clothes, which could not be gotten forth but by force, yet afterwards would not depart from the dead corpse, but came and lay between her head and her shoulders.'

The date of the first appearance of the breed in England is in some doubt, but it is generally thought that originally it was Japanese and was taken from that country to Spain. Wherever it came from, its tremendous popularity with King Charles II certainly made it one of the most important of the toydogs from very early times in England.

At one time the breed was so distinguished by colour that it was divided into separate varieties, the Blenheims of Marlborough, once known as the Marlborough spaniel, and a rich orange-and-

(*facing page*) King Charles spaniel

white mixture; the King Charles, which was black and tan; the Prince Charles which was a tricolour; and the ruby spaniel which, as its name implies, was a rich unbroken red in colour. Now they are all classified together and one standard of points serves for the whole breed. It is interesting that the docking of tails is now optional although, as evidenced by early paintings and even those as recent as Sir Edward Landseer (1802–73), the tail was originally left long, well-feathered and flowing.

They have the same sort of appeal as their larger cousins, the spaniels proper – luminous eyes and low-slung ears, and their habit of quietly fawning on human beings. They have retained something of the elegance and courtliness that they must have had in their early days to be so completely accepted as part of the court. They condescend to a certain extent, enjoying a fuss but making it quite clear that they are permitting rather than demanding it. Their sweetness, their essentially correct manners, the fact that they will not intrude but will make themselves quite independently comfortable in another part of the room and their lack of bad habits make them one of the most acceptable of house pets.

At the same time they have retained a good deal of their sporting instincts. They are after all spaniels, and nothing gives them greater pleasure than exploration, burrowing among the undergrowth of a garden after signs of small game or chasing round the countryside on the scent of rabbits and larger animals. Their flowing plumes and dramatic appearance, the fact that they will not chase farm animals, are easily trained to return on command and will walk at heel easily enough, all combine to make them ideal dogs for walks in the country.

Cavalier King Charles

The Cavalier King Charles spaniel is an offshoot from the confusion that existed in the breed of toy spaniels up to the early part of this century, and owes its existence to one enthusiast in the USA who was so impressed by the differences that old paintings showed between the sixteenth- and seventeenth-century King Charles spaniels, that he was determined that they should be resurrected as a separate breed. The main difference was in the head, with its longer face, flat skull, no dome, no stop, and a coloured spot in the middle of the skull. In the early part of this century special prizes were offered for dogs of this type. The attempt was so successful that a breed club was formed in 1928 and the Cavalier King Charles spaniel as we know it today was confirmed as a separate breed. Apart from the detailed differences, the Cavalier is much the larger of the two, with a maximum desirable weight of 18 lb (8·2 kg) as against 14 lb (6·4 kg) for the King Charles spaniel, which makes it one of the heavyweights of the toydogs.

The Cavalier has made tremendous strides in popularity in recent years. It was already increasing quite remarkably when a few years ago one succeeded in becoming champion of champions at Crufts, a feat not performed before by one of the breed. The resultant publicity caused a major upsurge in sales and interest, and the breed now heads the toydog entry at many of the world's major dog shows.

(*facing page*) Cavalier King Charles spaniel

Japanese

The other toy breed with something of the spaniel look about it is Japanese, but unless one accepts that the spaniels that produced the Cavalier King Charles and the King Charles spaniel themselves had some oriental connection, the relationship must be very remote. Even so the temperament of these little dogs is much the same as the other spaniel types in the group, with the same sort of appeal in their large dark eyes and pendant ears. It is when they move that the real difference shows, as while the other spaniels move more slowly and with a less confident look, the Japanese is gay, lively and high-stepping, with more of the smartness of the Pomeranian about its general outlook.

They are most affectionate, as would be expected of so small a dog, with a size and weight comparable to that of a Pomeranian. They have something of the appeal of a mischievous child, demanding attention and responding to it in a quick alert way that is most entertaining. Yet once they are in the show ring they seem to realise what is going on and they adopt a cloak of dignity that makes them ideal for this purpose.

They are on the other hand less hard, more expressive and quieter than some spaniels. They are perky enough and their expression is lively and alert, their sparkling dark eyes and picturesque large long-fringed ears giving them a look of understanding. Yet they are sturdy enough in spite of their small size and very obvious elegance, and it is easy to be misled into thinking that they are far more delicate than they really are. They have a silky well-groomed look about them which belies their strength of character as they are loyal friends, very much the family dog, and attached to one place and one family rather than to one particular person. In many ways they are the true toydog as they enjoy taking part in family games, especially when small children are also involved, and are happy showing off jewelled collars and fancy leads. They will even enjoy being treated as a doll and being dressed up by the children.

It has been claimed that the description of Japanese is misapplied to the breed, and that its origin lies in China rather than Japan. However, in Vero Shaw's book of 1881 it appears among the listed foreign dogs as a Japanese pug, and is described as not unlike our modern toy spaniels in general outline, being coated and feathered and generally black and white in colour, which is an apt description of the breed. One was shown at Alexandra Palace in 1881 in the toy spaniel class.

The modern history of the breed began in 1853 when a seafarer, a Commodore Perry, travelling to the Far East on a quest to open up trade, was presented with a pair of Japanese spaniels. It seems to have been a habit in those early days to give dogs to visitors as a mark of respect, and fortunately for us they survived the somewhat uncomfortable and dangerous journeys back to this country and, in many instances, formed the basis of our stock. In this case Perry presented his pair to Queen Victoria, whose patronage, combined with the appeal of anything oriental at that time, ensured the increased popularity of the breed.

(facing page) Japanese

Papillon

While the miniature pinscher came to us from Germany with perhaps a touch of English and Dutch about it, the papillon almost certainly started life in Spain as the continental toy spaniel. Sometimes known as the butterfly dog because of the shape of its ears with their long feathering and the way in which they are carried erect, the fact that it was named in French is probably due to its being popular as a breed with the ladies of the French court, Madame de Pompadour having one, as did Marie Antoinette.

They were at one time known as squirrel spaniels, not for any reasons connected with hunting but because the way in which they carry their heavily plumed tail over their back is reminiscent of a squirrel. There is a variety of the same animal, called the phalene and popular on the continent. This dog is so called because while the papillon carries its ears erect, the phalene carries them folded down like the wings of a moth. They are seen frequently in France, but have not become as popular as the papillon in England.

Papillons have been bred away from the other spaniels in appearance, and the papillons proper (as distinct from the flop-eared variety, the phalenes, with their distinctive large prick ears and heavy feathering) are very little like spaniels as we know them. They are elegant and graceful, with a coat, style and comportment that distinguishes them from all the other breeds. They have been bred to look well, and this has been done remarkably successfully. They have a proud bearing, carrying their tails well over their backs when moving smartly round on a lead, and even in play they have a gracefulness that is most enjoyable to watch. They are very light on their feet, do not normally put on much weight, and carry themselves as well in maturity and even in old age as they do when they are youngsters. In addition they are very flashy and showy, beautifully marked in a variety of colours and patterns, and seen together in a group, either resting in a variety of attractive poses or moving rapidly and gracefully across a lawn, they remind one forcibly of a miniature pack of borzois.

There is no vice about papillons. Generations of being kept as house pets, with all the care and attention that that implies, has resulted in a dog that exemplifies the whole idea of a toydog. They are fearless, but will never seek a fight; inquisitive, but quite capable of keeping out of trouble; and mischievous without being destructive. As show dogs they are quite remarkable, having great confidence in the ring, and it is not unusual to see a dozen or more papillons parading around, all full of confidence, all trying their best to look attractive and all obeying the gestures of their handlers. This is equally true of them in France, where they are shown in quite large numbers, being a very popular breed, and where too they have this air of quiet and elegant confidence. They are equally sweet-tempered and quite delightful to have around the house, enjoying life yet being unobtrusive when required to be and playful when their owner feels like indulging them.

Possibly papillons have a kind of extra-sensory perception, some sense that warns them of danger or of events that either have happened or are about to happen. Elsie Old, who lives in Oxford, tells the story of her papillons and their reactions to some power or influence that was not felt by her but which was clearly vivid to the dogs. It appears that a few years ago Oxford City Council began a large new development which entailed pulling down and digging up a large part of the old city. Of course, Oxford is a very old city and there have almost certainly been some strange happenings at times in its narrow streets and old houses.

One of the areas that was designated for demolition was the site of the old Grey Friars Settlement, and during the excavations that followed the demolition of the old buildings a number of

(facing page) Papillon

interesting archaeological finds were made, including two very ancient skeletons lying in a shallow grave. So much interest was shown in them that the area was roped off to allow those who so wished to walk round and view them. Elsie Old joined the sightseers, and took with her two of her papillon dogs that were noted for their extrovert character and were very accustomed to walking the streets of Oxford. While she was looking at the remains she suddenly looked down at the two dogs, both of which were showing every evidence of extreme fear, being tucked up and shaking, with their tails clapped right underneath. Normally happy dogs, cheerful and unafraid, they walked up to the site quite happily but were suddenly stricken with an immense dread.

Another owner of the breed, Mrs Alger, tells similar stories about her dogs. She had been accustomed to keeshounds and Alsatians among others, intelligent if much larger dogs, and she finds papillons very different. She says that they are always one jump ahead, even knowing which room you are going in next. This suggests that papillons may have some psychic gift.

Another story concerns Mrs Alger. When she had her first papillon she was living in a small seventeenth-century cottage in Salisbury and her husband was working in London, only managing to get down to Salisbury for occasional weekends. One Sunday morning at 10am Robin, her papillon, seated himself at the front door and refused to move. Two hours later her husband arrived unexpectedly, having boarded his train in London at exactly 10am. No one knew that he was coming, and yet the papillon was waiting for his master from the moment he left London. The next time that Robin did the same thing, Mrs Alger was so certain that her husband was coming on the same train that she even set an extra place for lunch. When the dog did not wait on the step, Mrs Alger knew that her husband was not coming; but when Robin did she knew for certain that her husband was going to arrive.

Robin also seemed to be aware of presences that no one else could see or sense. He would go up to 'someone' in the house, particularly in the bedroom, jump up to knee height, licking and turning round trying to understand why mere humans could not see the person that he was greeting. He would follow this invisible someone round a room in just the same way as he did a human being, and always seemed puzzled that no one reacted. Mrs Alger was never worried by this presence as she always felt that whatever or whoever it was must be quite pleasant as Robin was always most selective about his friends.

Papillons seem to be capable of facing up to unfamiliar situations with a considerable amount of equanimity. Mrs Alger stayed with a colonel and his wife at their large country house while on their way to the Paignton Championship Show. She had her two papillons with her as usual, one of them being Robin, mentioned above. The colonel had a large flock of geese in a huge paddock and because Robin had been described as being completely fearless he picked him up and dumped him in with the geese, saying 'that'll settle him'. Not at all, Robin immediately set to work just like a miniature sheepdog, rounded up the geese in the approved manner, nipping the heels of the recalcitrant ones, and eventually driving them all up into a corner of the paddock, where he held them until they had to be rescued by a somewhat red-faced colonel. The dog that captured the imagination of the public in recent years was the Yorkshire terrier that reached the finals of the obedience championships at Crufts, but with pugs that can be trained to a high level of efficiency and papillons that can round up geese it is obvious that toydogs are not just pretty faces.

(facing page) Japanese

6
OTHER TYPES

Pomeranian

From time to time we have been guilty of misnaming breeds of dogs. It happens that someone imports a breed, known in small numbers in one country, jumps to the conclusion that it is and always has been a native of that country, and promptly names it after the place where it was found, ignoring the fact that a little research would reveal that for some ethnic reason that particular breed had moved from say one part of Europe to another.

The Pomeranian is a typical example of this. It is unlikely that the breed as we know it today came in fact from Pomerania. The situation regarding the spitz breed is confusing as in one form or another this type of dog has existed for centuries in many different parts of the northern hemisphere. The Pomeranian as we know it is a typical spitz dog in spite of its lack of size. It is allied to the keeshound, the Finnish spitz, and all those prick-eared, curly tailed, thick-coated breeds that are spread from China to Alaska.

Dogs of the spitz type have been found depicted on ancient artifacts, as indeed dogs of so many types have. It is easy to interpret these often somewhat vague drawings and engravings as being almost any breed of dog and to use this as a evidence for the existence of a particular breed in very early times. In fact there are early examples of a spitz type of dog which are easily recognisable as such, but it would be an error to claim that this proves the existence of Pomeranians in the pre-Christian era.

In the early days of dog shows, Pomeranians were much bigger than they are now, weighing up to 20 lb (9·1 kg), and there was no mention of the size in the standard. Now the accepted size is from 4–5½ lb (1·8–2·5 kg). Colour too has changed. Whilst any whole colour is allowed, the once-popular white has disappeared

(*facing page*) Bichon frise

GLOVER

and most that are seen today are sable, red and cream, and orange. It is interesting that a breed of white dog still exists that is very like a Pomeranian, oddly enough in Ceylon for one place, where they are known as Japanese spitz.

It is a fairly simple matter to reduce a breed of dog in size, but it is not nearly so easy to change its character. The Yorkshire terrier, while developed as a toy, was produced from terriers and retains the characteristics of that breed. The Italian greyhound although no longer used for chasing game, was bred from dogs that did and as a result still retains the instinct to do so. The Pomeranian was originally a large working dog, probably used for herding, and the instincts of a herding and working dog are very different from those of a companion dog. The result of this is that although Pomeranians have the instinct to seek human companionship that all dogs have, they do not have the same approach to living with people as do some of the other toy breeds.

They are noisier than most, and tremendous guards of property and people. Their instinct to protect territory is developed to a high degree, and they will bark at the slightest sign of intruders at any hour of the day or night, and will often continue to bark until all apparent danger is long past. They are bold to a remarkable extent and will stand up to the biggest dog that they meet, defying mastiffs and Great Danes in the show ring in a manner that completely belies their very small size. They are small and very fine-boned, with tiny heads and feet, and to see a Pomeranian challenging something fifty times as large is one of the more amusing sights of a modern dog show.

If there is one thing that Pomeranians have above all else, it is style. They have a head start in that most of the larger dogs in the spitz family have this quality. When standing alert, with head up gazing into the distance, and with tail curled well over the back, there is no finer picture of a stylish dog than a member of the spitz breed. Although reduced in size, they have gained rather than lost in smartness and alertness. They stand in the show ring with their heads well back, their ears pricked, looking usually upwards or straight ahead at another dog, and when they are pleased their tails are carried right over their backs, giving a short sharp outline that is not bettered by any other breed.

Pomeranians have the power of possession. Owners who have had them say that they don't own the dogs, the dogs own them. It is something to do with the extremely close association that they develop with places and people, and something to do with the fact that of all the breeds, they are the real sleeve dogs. There is something about the shape of Pomeranians that lends them to being carried over the arm in a very individual way. They are something of a front-emphasis dog with small hindquarters and a large and luxurious ruff around the neck which makes it possible for them to be held in the curve of an elbow while the arm is still left virtually free. It is not unusual to see a lady out shopping managing her basket, handbag and umbrella and with a Pomeranian looped quite happily over one arm.

As with so many of the spitz breeds they are sharp, in temperament, but they will not fight unless provoked, and are remarkably good watchdogs, possessing a loud clear voice that they will use quite frequently to announce anything untoward. As has been said, they are very territory-conscious, and it is likely that when they are being defensive they are making sure that their basket is not being attacked, just as much as they are defending a household.

They are obedient little dogs, learning the sounds of words very quickly, and while they love exploring, they are usually under command and will return when called. They are sharp in character as well as appearance, but this is not to say that they are nasty tempered; in fact they are most affectionate with their owners and very good with children.

(*facing page*) Pomeranian

Italian Greyhound

The Italian greyhound is one of the really ancient breeds in the toydog group. Down the centuries they have graced just about all the palaces of the royal families in Europe. Dogs which are undoubtedly Italian greyhounds are depicted in many of the early Italian paintings. Some claim that they are whippets, but the whippet is a much later production in England and there is no doubt that they are these tiny greyhound running dogs.

The first mention of the breed in an English book is in the *Sportsman's Repository* of 1820, and is in fact one of only two toy breeds mentioned. There it is stated that they were probably brought over from Italy in the reign of Charles I and became a favourite of the ladies of the court in the following reign.

There is a story of the famous highwayman Duval who, failing to get his usual loot when stopping the Duchess of Portsmouth, one of the mistresses of Charles II, took instead the Italian greyhound that was riding on the box with the coachman. The incident developed all the constituents of the hijack as Duval later demanded 100 pieces for the return of the dog, which was agreed to, and the dog was given back to the duchess.

Although definitely toydogs, Italian greyhounds are not just over-pampered, spoiled and useless creatures. They retain much of the coursing instinct that their shape would denote belongs to them, and in Europe they are raced on a circular track in much the same way as their larger cousins, the whippets and the greyhounds proper. Nor are they nearly as fragile as their fine bones would suggest. Indeed one of the author's took fright at a vacuum cleaner being switched on behind her and leapt out of a first-floor window some 15ft to the grass below with no damage or injury. In character the Italian greyhounds are very much like whippets, being something of a mixture. At one moment they will be accepting petting and endearments as though they were not dogs

at all, and the next they will be flying off in pursuit of something which if small enough and if they catch it, they will definitely kill. Their favourite quarry is small birds, and they will rush out into a flock of sparrows, leaping high in the air and not infrequently succeeding in their attempts to catch one.

The Yorkshireman, who has a soft spot for a whippet, has a word for the temperament of the breed, which could just as well be applied to the Italian greyhound – they say that they are 'maungey'. There may be no exact equivalent for this very ancient dialect word, but it means miserable without being unhappy, completely dependent and hanging on every word, anxious always to do the right thing in order to please. Italian greyhounds are like that.

They are not effusive and fussy, yet attach themselves to one person to the exclusion of all others, following that person around constantly and, if there are a number of them, crying for his affection. It is this characteristic more than any other that has endeared them especially to the ladies as a pet and companion of the bedchamber. They appear to be completely random in their choice of friends, scorning one who they have known for years and falling completely for another that they only see at very infrequent intervals. Many of the running dogs are like this, seeming to see in one completely innocuous person a potential enemy and yet making great friends with another whose temperament and approach appears to us to be identical.

For the owner who wants a small dog, one that takes up very little space in house or car, yet a dog with highly developed sporting instincts and that will respond to exercise, grooming and fitness training, there could be little better than an Italian greyhound. They give a great deal of pleasure, will become very attached, and their graceful beautifully muscled appearance is something to be proud of.

(*facing page*) Italian greyhound

Pearce

Bichon Frise

One of the oldest-known of the toydogs, the bichon frise, is enjoying a remarkable revival. It has been known, although perhaps not by this name, in Europe for a great number of years, appearing in old paintings as a very small stockily built dog covered in masses of long curly white hair. They are said to have descended from the old French water dog, the Barbet, from which others in the group almost certainly also were bred. The bichon à poil frisé, to give it its full name, cropped up in Tenerife in the nineteenth century but the FCI recognised it as a Franco-Belgian dog, while its close cousin, the bichon Bolognese, was recognised as Italian.

The breed achieved some popularity in the USA after World War II, and was then introduced into Great Britain where it is rapidly gaining favour among those who want a small attractive dog with a delightful temperament and which looks a little different from other dogs in the group.

(*facing page*) Bichon frise

Italian greyhound

7
GENERAL CARE AND ATTENTION

One of the first things to appreciate about toydogs is that they are not naturally delicate just because they are small, but they are just as hardy as other breeds of dog. After all, the climate in that part of the British Isles that has produced more miniaturised animals than most, the Shetland Isles, is probably the most severe that the country experiences. For quite a large part of the year the Shetlands have snow, frosts and high winds, yet the Shetland sheepdog and pony both originated there.

Housing

Most toydogs are kept indoors, but this is largely convention. They are small, and have been bred as companions for generations with the purpose of making them suitable for keeping in a house. It is natural, therefore, to look upon them as house dogs rather than as kennel dogs, but there is no reason why they should not live in kennels as larger dogs do if there is good reason why they should. Most kennels these days are well-equipped heated dog houses, and the old-fashioned crude wooden structures that at one time served have to a large extent disappeared. With new legislation about kennel conditions and the breeding of dogs, many unsuitable dog houses which still remain will probably soon disappear.

It is necessary, however, to remember that toydogs are essentially companion dogs, and that they only flourish when they are constantly in the company of people. Left to their own devices or to the company of one another they would probably be perfectly happy, but they would not blossom into the intelligent, friendly little creatures that they are when kept in the house.

So the first thing to consider is how they should be housed. It is not enough to say that they are in the house. A house belongs

(*facing page*) Miniature pinscher

GLOVER

to human beings, although there is many a toydog that would dispute that, as they seem to take the house over once they get a foothold. Even when they live in the house, they still need accommodation which they can think of as their own. Ideally this should be a separate house within the house, and providing that the building is spacious enough some excellent arrangements on this basis can be made. A room or part of the house can be given over to the dogs, a place where they can be kept, fed, groomed, bathed and where all their equipment from leads to trophies can be kept under the best possible conditions.

Above all else a toydog, and indeed any breed of dog, needs to be clean, and everything used by it and on it needs to be spotless. All grooming tools need constant attention, being washed after every time that they have been used, and kept under cover preferably in a cupboard designed for the purpose rather than just left lying about to collect dust and to deposit the dust that they have collected.

In former days people who kept horses always did this, and every country house of any size had its stables, with grooms' accommodation over, and above all, things like harness rooms and tack cupboards. Most people look upon dogs as so much smaller and therefore needing much less doing for them, but this is a false view of the problem. There is much more satisfaction in fitting out accommodation for the dogs in a well-organised manner, than in just allowing it to happen. In some countries the house for the dogs vies in luxury with that for the humans, and a great deal of pride is taken in the way in which the family dogs are looked after. On visiting dog breeders in many countries, you are more likely to be shown round the dog house than you are round the one used by the owners.

Much time, thought and money is put into the whole business of providing quarters for dogs who in this way achieve an importance that is denied them if they are just allowed to be around the house in a casual way. In addition to which it is not everyone who enjoys having dogs climbing around the furniture and making attempts to settle down on their knees. Socially it must be preferable to have the canine members of the family organised in such a way that they can be seen when wanted, and allowed to be by themselves when they want to be.

Toydogs fit into the domestic scene much more readily than most breeds, they are so much smaller for one thing, but that apart they are temperamentally better suited to spending their time in the company of humans than many of the bigger dogs. Centuries of acceptance as part of the family has led them to feel that they belong in the house, and they respond to the domestic surroundings in such a way that they flourish both physically and mentally when they spend most of their time with the family.

There is no doubt too that they have a therapeutic effect on humans. They act as a sort of living 'worry beads' for one thing, as there is nothing more settling than to brush or stroke a dog – even its mere presence is helpful – when one is under some form of tension. In addition to this, the very fact that they are dependent upon humans is every bit as good for the states of mind of people as it is for the dogs'.

So, while it is better for the dogs to be housed in what the Americans would probably call custom-built accommodation, it is ideal if that accommodation is part of the house or closely attached to it so that there is constant contact between the dogs and the human inhabitants. There is no need for the dogs to be able to see people all the time, in fact it is probably better that they should not, but it is necessary that they should be able to both hear and smell them.

Sight is one of the less-important senses to dogs, they can in fact get along quite well without it, as has been seen many times, but they do depend on hearing, and to a much greater degree on scent. So long as dogs can hear people moving about (and their sense of hearing is so acute that they are capable of distinguishing one person's step from another and even one car engine from another), and so long as they can distinguish by scent who is still in the house, and within barking distance if needed, they are happy. The sensitivity of the dog's nose is something that is not understood by man, as the sense of smell in humans does not begin to approach it. It is only when someone has had personal experience of how powerful and accurate this sense is that the value of it is appreciated.

For instance, a Great Dane belonging to the author's father-in-law spent most of its time lying on the lawn in front of the house. At any time of day this dog would rouse himself, take a deep breath (with his nose in the air), and then set off to meet his master whom he would invariably greet more than halfway between the house and his place of work, the two being half a mile apart, the dog having picked up the scent as his master left the business and stepped out into the roadway. With this sort of scenting power it is very important that the place in which the dogs are housed should be reasonably adjacent to the house, and preferably joined to it.

Part of the joy of keeping any sort of animal is the pride of possession, and it is probably easier to be proud of a dog if it is in perfect condition. Conditioning is a matter of feeding, health, care and environment, and it is probable that the last of these is the most important. Environment governs the mental health and alertness of the dog as well as its physical well-being, and to surround a dog with everything that it can need for its physical comfort is to have won the battle against ill-health and mental dullness.

Everything in the dog house should be in first-class condition, grooming tools clean and put away, leads hanging on separate hooks, all feeding bowls perfectly clean and standing face down to keep them dust free. Owners should remember that dogs cannot provide for themselves in the civilised and sophisticated world that we have created. Their ancestors could provide their own homes, food and maternal care, but we have now accepted the responsibility of providing everything and we should see that everything is as near perfect as it possibly can be.

Toydogs need no more pampering than others. They get it, but only because owners prefer to treat them that way. Their lack of size, appealing approach to humans, and the fact that they make themselves very much part of the family, leads to them usually getting more attention. But it is no more true that they need special care than true they need coddling and spoiling. They are every bit as much dogs as their larger cousins.

Grooming

One of the most enjoyable things about toydogs is grooming them. They have between them the same diversity of coat as other breeds, the long silky hair of the Maltese, the wire coat of the griffon and the shiny smooth coat of the English toy terrier, but it is all on a much more manageable scale. Anyone who has faced up to the constant brushing and combing, as well as the bathing, of an Afghan hound, will know that detailed care of the sort needed on the scale of a dog of that size is a monumental task. It is rewarding, but extremely hard work. The coat of the Yorkshire terrier needs just the same treatment, and repays constant attention with a brush, but the scale is so much smaller that it ceases to be an apparently endless task and becomes a real pleasure. It compares with hoeing a row of carrots in one's own garden and doing the same thing across a 10 acre field.

For the sake of those who live in the house, as well as for anyone who visits, it is essential that toydogs kept in the house are clean. Dogs smell, which is a blunt way of saying that all dogs have a natural odour. Some people find it offensive, others do not mind

and some, especially those who have become hardened to it, seem to manage to ignore it. Toydogs have the same sort of natural smell as other breeds, it is handed down to them from their ancestors in the larger breeds. Some of the gundogs develop a natural oily smell, and many of the hounds have a natural doggy smell which can become offensive if allowed to permeate a house. Toydogs will develop the same sort of odour unless they are bathed regularly. This should be done as part of a regular routine of grooming if the dog is being shown, the bath will be part of the show preparation and the routine bathing will probably not be needed. The frequency of bathing will differ with every breed, long-coated dogs needing more bathing than short coats, and white dogs more than coloured, so that Maltese will need frequent washing not only to keep the coat clean but to ensure that it retains its sparkling whiteness.

There are a great many preparations marketed for the care of dogs' coats – conditioners, shampoos, oils and unguents of all sorts – but it is always as well to get expert advice from a breeder and exhibitor before deciding which one to use on a dog of any breed. It is worth remembering that the use of artificial colouring or texture aid is frowned upon if the dog is to be shown, and while it is perfectly legitimate to walk in the streets with a pink poodle, it does not do to enter the show ring with as much blue-rinse on the dog as you may have on your hair.

Some breeds need special coat care, especially if the dog is to be shown, and the Yorkshire terrier is a typical example. Left to itself, the coat of a mature Yorkshire terrier will grow until it reaches the floor, when constant friction will wear away the ends and it will grow no longer. If the dog is especially active the coat will never reach the floor as it will be pulled out in the rose bushes in the garden. Exhibitors of these little dogs have therefore adopted the expedient of fastening the coat up all round with pieces of paper or cloth and rubber bands to prevent this from happening, with the result that an exhibition Yorkie goes around the house looking like 'Little Annie Rooney' and metamorphoses from cocoon to butterfly only on show days.

Some of the short-haired dogs need little attention to coat. Miniature pinschers and English toy terriers can literally be picked out of the box at the last moment and popped into the show ring after only a brisk rub down with a smooth hound glove and a piece of chamois leather. Their coat condition comes from good health, and their coat will glow in the same way as does that of a racehorse paraded in the ring before a race, having had all possible care and attention lavished upon its physical condition for months beforehand. With the smooth-coated toydogs the dog must be healthy if the coat is to glow, and one of the first signs of illness in these breeds is when the coat begins to 'stare'.

Those breeds with wiry coats, such as the griffons, need the same attention as do the wire fox-terriers and Airedales. Left to grow, the coat will just go on getting longer until the animal is a rather shapeless mass of hair. By careful removal of the coat, mostly twice each year as the old coat is ready to come out naturally, the dog can be shaped to look much better than it will do in the rough. When preparing griffons for show the hair of their neck, back, hindquarters and back of forelegs needs to be trimmed out early in order to allow it to grow to the correct length before the show, while the remainder of the body is trimmed later to present it much shorter on the day of the show. All this is done with finger and thumb, as the coat must not be cut. Correctly done the shape of the animal can be emphasised, with the long stiff beard left on and the closely trimmed ears giving the correct griffon look.

(*facing page*) Showing how the King Charles spaniel has changed little in appearance over the centuries, a toy spaniel of 1850

Those breeds that have rather longer silkier coats need a certain amount of control too. The feathering on the ears and tail of papillons, and on the ears of Pekingese and King Charles spaniels, is a feature of those breeds and needs retaining and even encouraging as much as possible; but if left to its own devices, the coat will always grow where it is not wanted and will need to be reduced or removed. King Charles spaniels will grow furry heads, Pekingese will get hairy skulls, and elbows and ears will be emphasised when they should not be. By careful control of this, the animal can be improved; but it needs to be done very carefully, and at first under instruction, or the wrong part will be trimmed.

Those breeds with stand-off coats, like Pomeranians, need to grow as much coat as possible in order to give the trimmer something to work on. A long luxuriant coat can be shaped, but no one can put coat on where none exists. So the first principle is to grow the maximum coat by selective breeding and good diet, and to retain it by keeping the dogs under the best possible and cleanest conditions. The trimming of Pomeranians takes a great deal of skill. The shaping of the tail, the contouring of the whole animal to give it the rounded effect that is needed, and the delicate trimming of surplus hair from the ears to shape them and yet leave them looking as though they are natural all takes time and expertise, and again needs training.

One of the great advantages of toydogs is that, being small, they are easily handled, and at no time is this more obvious than when bathtime comes round. All dogs need a bath occasionally, even if it is only a plunge in a neighbouring stream or the sea, but dogs that live in the house, or at least in close contact with humans, need more frequent bathing for obvious reasons. Methods vary from breed to breed, but the principles remain the same. Some breeds need bathing less frequently (griffons for instance need less than others, and in fact some people say they need none at all, as it spoils the wiry quality of the coat), and some breeds, like Maltese, need bathing at least once a week, and more frequently if being exhibited, in order to retain the whiteness and improve the quality of the coat.

The principles are simple. In the first place use a type of shampoo that suits the coat of the dog, and this can best be discovered by asking someone with the experience of the breed. Never use the harsher forms of domestic detergent unless absolutely certain that they are harmless. The coats of the long-coated breeds should not be rubbed when washing or drying, but should be dealt with by brushing in the shampooing, rinsing and drying stages. This keeps the coat straight, and prevents tangles which can be difficult to remove and may destroy the coat.

The coats of Yorkshire terriers that are intended for exhibition are usually kept in what is called oil, except when actually being prepared for show or being shown. This oil is in fact any one of a whole number of oily mixtures, almost every exhibitor having his own favourite recipe, and is brushed into the coat as soon as the show is over and before the coat is tied up once again in cloth or paper strips. This presents certain difficulties when bathing the dogs, as every vestige of this oil must be removed before they are shown. In the first instance this is because it is against Kennel Club regulations to exhibit a dog with any foreign substance in its coat, and secondly because the full shining glow of the coat cannot be produced if any greasy substance is left in it. The lovely silken sheen of the coat of Yorkshire terriers is produced by good health, complete cleanliness and plenty of brushing.

Yorkshire terriers probably need bathing twice before a show, and drying between baths. Plenty of brushing at this stage will bring the last remains of the oil out of the skin and the second

(*facing page*) Group composed of English toy terrier, Yorkshire terrier and Italian greyhound from a coloured engraving by A F Lydon 1889

wash will remove all traces. The coat is fairly fragile, and every effort must be made to avoid using any substance for washing which will destroy the quality. If a dryer is used it must never be brought into close contact with the coat as this will cause overdrying and destruction of the natural structure of the hairs themselves.

Constant attention to detailed cleanliness is important with little dogs. The bigger breeds take more rough and tumble exercise, they rub around, have a good scratch, chew branches off trees and wear their toenails down on rough ground. Not every smaller dog will do all of these things and some attention from the owner is needed. Skin care is important, and the natural stroking that goes on as the toydog is nursed is one of the best ways of ensuring this. A lazy skin is usually an unhealthy one, collecting dead hair follicles and dust, and the best way of ensuring a completely healthy skin is with massage. With a big dog this is often an undertaking, and a racing greyhound will have its daily massage session with a kennel man just to keep the skin healthy and to tone up the muscles. With a toydog this gets done quite incidentally as the dog sits on a knee being fussed, a process which the dog enjoys every bit as much as the owner. It is all part of the mutual admiration that goes on between dog and owner.

Teeth in the smaller breeds do present a problem. Good sound teeth are important to the health of the dog. At one time, when feeding was more natural, they were vital, but now, with carefully contrived compounds, good teeth are not so essential. Some of the toy breeds keep their teeth well, although some, and Yorkshire terriers are a typical example, do not. It is not unusual to find a Yorkshire terrier of six or seven years of age with hardly a tooth left. Regular cleaning will help, and the removal of tartar from the areas between the teeth and close to the gums will prevent a good deal of decay that will otherwise occur. Dogs sometimes object to this being done, but like everything else, if it is started when the dog is young and carried out regularly, it is accepted.

Toydogs need their nails trimming regularly, and it is not possible to take short cuts. The nail session should become a weekly affair even if there does not appear at first that there is much nail to be removed. The centre of the dogs' nail consists of the quick, and in neglected nails this grows as long as the nails themselves, which will mean that if eventually the nail needs taking well back the quick will be cut into and will be painful to the dog. If the nails are kept short the quick will not grow, and nail trimming does not become the torture that the dog always seems to think it is going to be.

There are many ways of trimming nails, but only one correct way, and that is best learned from an expert. A little training and the right type and size of clipper for the job, and the weekly nail drill becomes nothing of a trial at all. Some breeds wear their nails down in the course of exercise, but it is best not to allow nature to take its course as little bumps and injuries will cause a dog to favour one foot or some toes, and this will in its turn lead to uneven growth of nails which again leads to more uneven walking and eventually the dog will get into very bad walking habits, something which is especially frowned upon in the show ring.

Feeding

Animal diet is in itself a complicated study, but fortunately most of the work has already been done by the manufacturers of dog foods. Teams of scientists have made a detailed study of the whole question of what is healthy food for dogs, and most of the concern over feeding and the hard work of food preparation has been removed from our shoulders. There are, however, one or two common misunderstandings about the diet of dogs which need to be cleared up before considering the details of how individual dogs should be fed.

The first misnomer to be dealt with is the association of dog feeding with human diet. In fact, the sort of food that we eat is *not* suitable for dogs. They will eat it and love it, but the fact remains that it is not healthy food for them. The standard reply that veterinarians get when they ask an owner of an overweight dog what it eats is that it gets just the same as its master gets, an answer offered with all the pride of doing the best for the animal. In fact this is probably one of the worst ways of feeding a dog, usually indicating unsuitable food given at the incorrect times. Dogs are natural carnivores, but they also are natural scroungers as well. In the wild state they would be almost entirely eaters of flesh and some herbs, but when domesticated they are swallowers of cream cakes, chocolate and ice cream.

Owners sometimes also make the mistake of feeding their dog too frequently. The over-indulgent owner feels that the poor thing is hungry and feeds it at almost any hour of the day; and when the owner is one member of a family of several the cunning dog will always trick any member of the family who happens to be eating something into believing that it has had nothing to eat for days. In fact a hungry dog is usually a healthy dog – hungry as distinct from starving – and many expert owners 'treat' their dogs to one foodless day per week. In its natural state the wild dog hunts once during the day, usually towards dusk, fills its stomach and spends the night sleeping off the effects. To be sampling all sorts of mixed bits of food all day is as unnatural to a dog as it is unhealthy.

There is an old-wives' tale which holds that raw meat is bad for dogs. Nothing could be further from the truth. Raw meat is the natural food of the whole canine race, and whilst it is not essential for a dog to have a proportion of raw meat in its diet, it can do it no harm and is likely to do good. Many experts on the rearing of dogs from puppyhood will say that a puppy should have some finely scraped or minced raw meat as soon as it is weaned. This is natural too, as the earliest solid food that a puppy will get in the wild state is thoroughly chewed and swallowed meat regurgitated by the mother.

The best food for baby puppies is their mother's milk, and there is no perfect substitute for it. There are a good many proprietary puppy milk foods on the market which will in an emergency prove quite adequate and which are used extensively by dog breeders to supplement the milk of the mother when that proves inadequate. Puppies can be taught to lap at a very early age by holding a dish of milk near to them and allowing them to lick a finger dipped into it. It takes only minutes to teach them to do this, but the same rule applies here as with feeding at any other time during the life of the dog – that overfeeding is more dangerous than underfeeding. The puppies should be allowed to feed and then to sleep.

In the case of the tiny puppies of some of the toy breeds, when the dam is incapable for some reason of feeding the puppies naturally then artificial feeding has to be resorted to. Some of the puppies are so small that even the tiniest feeding bottle is too large, but it is possible to feed with a dropper, the sort of thing that can be found in bottles of eye lotion or which at one time were used for filling pens. It needs a great deal of patience, but in the case of valuable puppies it is clearly worthwhile.

Once weaning time is past, and the usual signs of this are that the dam will try to feed the puppies some of her food, then the real work of feeding starts for the owner. The dam will go on feeding the puppies for some time after they have started to take solid foods. There is no harm in this unless it goes on too long and the dam loses weight, or if she is needed back in show condition quickly, when she can be removed from the puppies more or less permanently, only being allowed to see them at infrequent intervals. The dam herself will govern the frequency as she will at this stage begin to lose interest and will make her calls less and less frequently until she eventually gives them up altogether.

Advice on puppy feeding is readily available. Most of the manufacturers of puppy food and dog food generally publish leaflets on the subject. Naturally enough they are geared to their own products, but the general principle is the same for all of them. Puppy meal and biscuit is produced in quantity and there is great competition for the vast market that exists. Compound foods that contain all the protein, carbohydrates and additives that are needed are readily available these days, and it is just a question of personal choice.

If the number of puppies in a litter is large, supplementary feeding may be needed, and there are many milk foods developed for young puppies that can be used. The choice is between one of those specially developed for puppies or one of the standard milk foods produced for human consumption. Those fortunate enough to be able to procure goats' milk will use that as just about the best substitute for bitches' milk, and some dog breeders keep goats for just that purpose. At the initial stages feeding must take place at two hourly intervals, but after the first week the food can be gradually increased and the intervals extended, until at three weeks a little scraped raw meat can be introduced.

By four or five weeks the raw meat can be given twice daily and that, alternated with milk food and such solid food as Farex, will make up the five or six feeds per day that the puppies need. By eight weeks the number of feeds can be reduced to four, with perhaps a drink last thing at night. In addition water should be available at all times. By three months of age the number of feeds can be reduced to three, and by the time that the puppy is six months' old it will be happy on two feeds per day.

There has always been some controversy about the number of times an adult dog should be fed during the day and at what time that feeding should take place. Opinions vary from the hunt kennelman, who will toss a carcass into the pack and allow them to eat as and when they will, to the scientific, who will persuade a veterinarian to prepare a diet sheet for individual dogs. The old-fashioned dog breeder, who kept dogs long before the development of modern scientifically compounded foods, will still feed once per day, usually in the evenings. He will prepare his feeds from meat and biscuit meal with the addition of some vegetables as he always has done. Many with shorter experience will depend on compounded and tinned foods and will get results which are probably just as good.

The short answer is probably that it is a matter of choice on how a dog is fed – dictated by economics, fashion and convenience. If you happen to live on a farm there is nothing better for dogs, especially young dogs, than milk and eggs. If you happen to be a butcher, or know one well, then fresh meat will be the mainstay of your dog's diet. If you live in the middle of a town, surrounded by pet shops and supermarkets, then most of the food will come out of tins and plastic bags.

(facing page) Pug

8 EDUCATION AND SHOWING

Development

I hesitate to use the term 'training' when speaking of toydogs as they are so intelligent that they respond better to education than they do to the routine of training. 'Training' brings to mind a long period of repetition of dull routine exercises until they become a habit. With toydogs this is not necessary, as their reactions to instructions are more rapid than with many dogs, and when they understand what is required they will do it because they enjoy doing it and not because they feel that they have to.

The development of a puppy is remarkably fast. Once it has its sight, the other faculties follow along very quickly, and the tiny helpless baby that was entirely dependent upon its mother very suddenly develops independence and a will and character of its own. Some will show signs of wilfulness whilst others will appear reserved, and the timing of their education can be adjusted to the temperament that each is developing. If a puppy is intended for showing, its education cannot begin too early. Once the eyes are open and it begins to understand that it is to be part of a human as well as a canine family, its learning can begin. At first this will consist purely and simply of handling, teaching it that there is nothing to fear in being passed from hand to hand, of being fondled, and even of being asked to stand and sit still for a while.

Whippets are probably the supreme example of a breed that takes naturally to being exhibited, and when I was breeding them baby puppies were being handled and even stood on flat surfaces before their eyes were completely open. They were held regularly right from the moment of birth, and neither they nor the dam ever appeared to object. That is not to say that baby puppies should be handled by anyone at an early age. They should be protected from the over-attention of children for instance, as this early

(facing page) Pomeranian

contact will have a great deal to do with their temperament in later life and is something that should only be done by an expert. It is at this stage that they will gain confidence and they should be handled with extreme care in order to avoid any loss of that confidence in human beings. They will learn to appreciate that people are friendly and that they can be trusted, and it is at this stage that they should be talked to as much as possible in order that they should grow accustomed to the sound of human voices.

As soon as they begin to understand that human companionship is part of their future, they should be given a name and should be called and addressed by it at every opportunity. The uninitiated will find it difficult to understand how it is that dog breeders can distinguish one dog from another in a litter, all of which are superficially alike, but there are subtle differences which those who are in constant contact with the dogs recognise immediately; and it is not difficult to give each puppy a distinctive short name that is soon recognisable to it. The long and sometimes complicated registered name comes later, but this name can stay with the dog all its life as its pet name.

So the first lesson is on its way, the puppy learns its name and needs to reach the stage when it comes on call. This can best be done by reward. A puppy will learn quickly that when it hears its name an attractive morsel of food follows automatically, and once the lesson is learned the food incentive can be dropped in favour of a little petting. A considerable amount of patience is needed at this stage as there will be moments when the puppy is engaged on attractive little investigations of its own, and will not want to leave them. It is destructive at this stage to scold when this happens, and the person who is doing the teaching needs to have the patience (and the time) to continue calling and encouraging the dog to return until it eventually comes.

A puppy's life at this time is governed by cause and effect, and its active little brain will associate certain actions with certain reactions very quickly. If it returns any one time to a scolding, its confidence in what it has already learned is devalued and it can be slow to recover. The whole process of education is based upon mutual trust and confidence. With puppies it is a matter of common sense and of the teacher, in most cases the owner, trying to think as the puppy is thinking and attempting all the time to relate the next lesson to what has been learned so far and the amount of progress that the puppy has made.

It is one of the rules of the Kennel Club that a dog must be shown on a lead when in the ring, so if the puppy is eventually to become a show dog it must be taught to walk and stand on the end of a lead. This is not difficult if it is approached in the right way. Puppies object to wearing a collar and will usually sit and scratch as soon as one is placed round their neck. If they relate it to something enjoyable such as play, they soon grow accustomed to it. The best way is probably to put a very light collar on them just before they are let out for a romp in the garden, when they will be so interested in everything else that is going on that they will for a while forget that they are wearing a collar. The length of the lesson can be gradually extended until they will look forward to having the collar put on and will wear it quite happily.

The next lesson is that the collar can be used as a form of restraint, and this can prove a little difficult sometimes. Puppies enjoy their freedom and object to anything that limits it. In an extreme case they will even become aggressive. Here is where human cunning can settle the problem. Once he has grown accustomed to the collar a light lead can be attached to it and the puppy allowed to move freely, dragging the lead around for a while, feeling only the restriction of the weight of the lead itself. From that to the next stage of having someone hold the other end of the lead is an easy one, and in a very short time the puppy will accept the fact that he is attached to his master and can only go where he wishes to go.

All this must be taught to the puppy before it ever enters the show ring, as in there there are so many other new experiences that it is unfair, and indeed rather stupid, to take an uneducated puppy into the ring on the basis of 'it will be all right on the night'. Nothing looks worse, is more embarrassing, or lowers the opinion of ringsiders, especially expert ringsiders, more quickly than someone trying to show a puppy that refuses to move, sits down, and generally gives the impression that it is the first time it has ever been out of the kennel. Some breeds learn more quickly than others, probably because some are more intelligent than others, although the advocates of those breeds which do not take too readily to lessons on lead and ring training will hasten to inform you that this is because they are too intelligent.

Some breeds are what is called 'biddable', which means docile and obedient, and is a quality that is not altogether typical of the toydogs. Some of them are inclined to be temperamentally that way, but the majority of them are far too ebullient and extroverted to be termed biddable. Instead they have an immense ability to respond to human beings and while they are docile, they are obedient, they do things because they know that it is the intelligent thing to do, not just because they feel that they should obey.

Exhibiting

Having gained the full confidence of a puppy and having managed to get it to accept collar and lead, it can then be introduced to the show ring. This is an experience that must be fairly terrifying to a small puppy. To be taken from the shelter of the family and to suddenly find itself in the centre of a mass of other dogs in a huge echoing smelly area must be nerve-wracking. This is where the preliminary education will prove its worth. For a while the puppy may show all the signs of being unhappy and disturbed, but if the teaching that has gone on so far has been the right sort

of instruction then he will soon remember that nothing has happened that has been unpleasant before and will gain confidence that it is not now about to happen. In a very short time he will be thoroughly enjoying the experience and displaying his charms just as he does at home. If he does not then the education is not complete and further ring experience should be deferred until more instruction has taken place at home.

An owner who is new to dog showing should visit several shows before venturing into the ring himself with a dog. There is a certain routine that is common to most shows, and although it differs in detail from one show to another in the main all shows are similar. It is not difficult to learn what goes on in the ring, and it is much better for an owner to know something of what is expected in order to prevent a situation in which both owner and dog are complete novices.

Toydogs are displayed on a table to begin with, and it is as well to accustom a puppy to stand on a table so that he does so without fear. If it is possible, at the same time get a friend to play the part of the judge and examine and handle it. This will make it understand that standing on a table is something which has a certain association with subsequent actions. It will make the puppy realise that the pattern of being shown holds no real terrors, and he will usually quite enjoy the experience. Toydogs are naturally friendly creatures, love having a fuss made of them, and will, as likely as not, end by licking the judge's face when they eventually do get to a show.

Once at a show, the dog should be encouraged to relax as much as possible. The bench, an essential part of the equipment of a show, or at least a large show, is in itself a barren uninviting sort of place, and one that the dog will not enjoy being placed in and at first certainly not being left in. It is essential that the immediate dog's surroundings should be made as familiar as possible. The best way of ensuring this is to have a special rug or blanket for the purpose of lining the cage, which is what a toydog bench really is, and that the dog should spend some time with this at home in order to grow accustomed to it. When it is new the dog should be allowed to sleep on it for a while, so that when it is taken to the show the dog remembers it as part of his usual environment and will sleep on it at the show just as he did at home. Many exhibitors go to great lengths to make the interior of the bench as decorative as possible, hanging curtaining, ribbons and frills round the cage in order to present a pretty picture. Although this is not in any way to be deplored, as it is all part of the presentation, at the same time it has to be accepted that it is this sort of thing that has led to much of the criticism that is levelled at the toydogs that they are useless pampered little darlings.

If the dog is allowed to relax until the time comes for it to be taken into the ring, it will generally wake up and display all the activity and liveliness that is wished. This should be encouraged. It has a parallel with conditions at home when the dog is wakened from its sleep in its usual place in front of the fire, or on the most comfortable armchair, and taken for a run round the garden. He grows accustomed to the idea that the transition from house to garden is similar to the one from cage to ring, and in the same way that he will show every sign of animation when he gets out of the house he will do the same when he is taken from his cage.

Dogs are creatures of habit, and if the correct habits are encouraged there should be no trouble with showing a dog. From the time that he settles in the car for his journey to the show to entering the hall, being groomed and prepared, being placed in his cage, then from there taken to the ring and placed on the table while strange hands pick him up and then ask him to walk in a certain way, the whole process can start off as a part of an education and finish up as a habit.

Dog shows are fun. Unless the exhibitor and the dog are both enjoying it, they would be better off at home. It is true that shows have become highly competitive and that winning can be very important, but losing can be important too, especially if it is accepted with good grace. If the dog has put on a good performance, has done just what has been asked of him and done it in the right spirit, he will have made just as many friends as if he had been declared the winner. Most of the people sitting at the ringside are experts in the breed that they are watching. Many of them will be looking for stock that they wish to buy or a dog that they wish to use at stud, and they are not just looking for the winner. They will be looking down the line for the sort of dog that they admire because his temperament is right or because he has certain physical or mental characteristics. If your dog happens to have those characteristics and if he has performed in a way that pleases, then he is likely to be as popular as if he had won everything available to him.

What is available to him? Shows are organised by bodies of people whose object is to promote the improvement of the pedigree dog and of dog shows, and in doing that they attempt to cater for everyone. Many of these bodies are breed clubs, established to look after the welfare of a particular breed. They organise shows, hold events other than shows, elect judges, establish the standard of their particular breed through the Kennel Club, and generally do everything that they can to further the interests not only of dogs but of owners and exhibitors.

Most of the toydog breeds have well-organised breed clubs which arrange shows up to championship level and it is not only possible, but advisable, for owners to take advantage of everything that the breed club offers in the way of activities and advice. Many produce regular editions of a club magazine, which will

(*facing page*) English toy terrier bitch from an old engraving by R H Moore late 19th century

89

contain a mass of useful information, everything from where the next show is to be to what exported dogs have been winning in other countries. Much valuable information concerning shows and other activities is contained in the pages of the journals produced for the dog owner. In these will be found dates of future shows, the results of past events, and breed notes containing useful data about all breeds.

A dog owner can enjoy meeting people with a common interest in a particular group of dog, and this can lead to a way of life that is not only pleasurable but can even become profitable. Most owners of toydogs will eventually find that they wish to begin breeding dogs, and the breed club and dog show provide the outlet and the shop window respectively. From small beginnings at one of the minor events that take place from time to time all over the country (such things as sanction shows or even exemption shows), an owner can progress up the ladder of success until the topmost rung is reached, at, say, a breed-club championship show. On the way he will make many friends, the sort who prove themselves helpful and generous, who will stand by in trouble and join in the celebration of success.

Owners of toydogs will soon learn that there is a particular camaraderie in the group. They tend to stick together because they have problems in common. They occupy a particular sort of bench, enjoy a closer-knit community in smaller rings and in the same way that their charges are defiant of bigger dogs, they tend to establish an attitude which protects them from the rough and tumble of the show. There is always a picnic atmosphere about the toydog benches at our bigger shows, with all the exhibitors chatting round their tables and exchanging anecdotes about their dogs and everyone else's. Toydogs have many advantages over the larger breeds. They are so small that transporting them to a show presents no problem. Where as another exhibitor can only take a couple of Great Danes in the back of the car, the toydog owner can take ten or a dozen of his dogs. One of the problems of entering dogs at a show is that of having a choice of several possible entrants. An exhibitor will choose perhaps two or at the most three if they are large dogs, and will probably find that it is just the ones that he left at home that will be the sort that the judge will prefer. With toys it is possible to take many more, thus increasing the possibility of success.

When travelling by public transport things are easier too. I remember catching a bus to a show in the immediate post-war period when conductors allowed only one dog per bus, and found myself sitting next to a lady who I knew as an exhibitor and who I suspected was going to the same show. She was having a quiet laugh at the antics of the conductor who did not allow on board anyone with a dog, as he already had an Alsatian on the back seat. She opened her shopping bag sufficiently wide for me to have a peep. She had two Yorkshire terriers dozing quietly in the bottom of it.

Most exhibitors of toydogs will take half a dozen to a championship show. They travel well in boxes, usually in pairs for company, and are remarkably quiet and well-behaved. When they arrive at the show, the boxes are transferred to a small wheeled vehicle and taken in this way direct to the benches.

Those who hold that there is something effeminate about a grown man playing around with tiny little dogs merely display by this attitude their lack of knowledge of the qualities of toydogs. They are certainly small, but they have as much personality as larger dogs, probably more, as they are highly intelligent, tremendously responsive and full of fun. Some are scornful at seeing exhibitors with their little carts loaded with boxes containing toydogs, but they forget that emperors, kings and princes have found them just as attractive.

Toydogs have a natural tendency to display themselves to advantage, they are natural extroverts and have a sparkle that none of the larger dogs seem to manage. Afghan hounds are every bit as glamorous as Japanese, yet while few Afghans sparkle in the ring, almost all Japanese do. Big dogs enter the show ring and stand in a certain way, move in a particular manner and generally behave as required simply because it is required of them, with the result that the compunction shows and when they get out of the ring their happy release from what to them has been something of a trial shows in their immediate relaxation and expressions of joy. Toydogs, on the other hand, show their pleasure at being in the ring. They make their way into the ring with an attitude of complete enthusiasm, a sort of 'I'm here, now what happens?' look about them, the eternal-child manner of freedom of expression that comes from real self-satisfaction.

One can watch a ring full of large dogs being coaxed into place with all their limbs in exactly the right relative positions, with exaggerated poses, tied up in front and propped up behind, often with a worried and weary expression on their faces as though they had seen it all before, which they probably have. When asked to move they go through the motions because they have been trained to do so but it is not a joyous performance, largely because such a display would be out of character for the breed in question. Toydogs, however, do not need either tying or propping, and most toydog rings avoid the look of a 'prayer meeting' such as one sees in many rings. Most of the breeds love to be in the ring and will show their enjoyment in a very obvious manner, looking round them with interest, fraternising with neighbours, paying attention to the girls, and generally making the most of themselves. If a miniature pinscher suddenly swaps ends because another dog is approaching too close, he does it in one quick jump, from one alert position 'statant guardant' to the same position as soon as he lands – and it simply does not matter, as he is showing himself to best advantage all the time. The same manoeuvre carried out by, say, an Old English sheepdog would throw the whole ring

into a state of confusion and dismay all the other dogs, his owner, himself and probably the judge as well.

Another of the great things about toydogs is the fact that they repay attention to their coats and appearance in a way that the larger dogs do not. There is something about bathing, grooming and shaping a Pomeranian, for example, that compares with putting the final touches to a piece of jewellery. The smaller scale of the dog seems to permit a greater degree of finish than is possible with bigger breeds. The same thing is true of poodles to a certain extent. The time spent in preparing a toy poodle compared with a miniature or a standard is generally about the same, but the very size of the bigger dog, and the sheer scope of the task usually results in a less-fine finish. Ten minutes spent polishing a Great Dane is lost on the sheer bulk of the beast, but the same ten minutes spent on the coat of an Italian greyhound will bring out the full sheen. The difference is comparable to that between the finish of a bowling green and that of a football pitch.

It is true that not all the breeds of toydog have the same amount of confidence and that puppies in most breeds will go through a stage of not enjoying the show ring, but in general the toydogs have this quality of inquisitiveness, alertness and showmanship that gives them the edge on all breeds from other groups. All this means that showing toydogs is in itself fun, and explains why there are as many men showing little dogs as there are large ones and why toydogs, although at one time very much the companions of the ladies, are not entirely their prerogative in the show ring.

In recent years it has become more common for children to handle dogs in the ring, and it is here that toydogs really come into their own. The showing of a dog is not just a matter of taking the end of the lead and marching into a ring hoping that everything will turn out well. It may do so, or it may be a disaster. The best guarantee against this happening is for a certain rapport between the handler and the dog, a complete understanding and respect for one another and pleasure at being in one another's company. For this to develop to the full it is important that the child should own the dog, should groom it, feed it and live with it, and the size alone of the toydogs, to say nothing of their delightful character, make them ideal dogs for children. The finest example of this man-animal relationship is, of course, that of the elephant and his mahout, who spend the whole of their lives together. In the early stages the mahout is only a child, but the elephant is also only in its infancy and as they grow up together even their thought processes seem to become entwined.

If one looks at old photographs of dog shows, the picture presented is that of a large number of tweedy, becapped and heavily whiskered men showing everything from bulldogs to greyhounds, and the very idea of a child entering the ring to join battle with them would have been abhorrent to many people. As things changed the tendency was for the child to be allowed to take a dog into the ring by kind permission of mama who was the palpable owner. Now children own dogs and show them, and what is more show them very successfully, competing against adults at the highest levels. This is a healthy revolution and one which almost everyone connected with dog showing, with the possible exception of those defeated by a child handler, will applaud.

One of the great pleasures of dog showing is that there are no barriers, the very young as well as the very old can participate and compete. People from all walks of life meet and compete with one another, swap stories almost as freely as they swap dogs, and although the sport is a great leveller, it is a levelling upwards rather than the other way. The old-timers are free with their advice and scenes at shows are often reminiscent of Millais' 'The Boyhood of Raleigh' as those with vast experience tell the youngsters what things were like in the 'good old days'.

(*facing page*) Lowchen

9
TOYDOGS IN ART

King Charles spaniel

Having spent a lifetime, or at least a professional lifetime, in the world of Art and having at the same time been deeply involved in the world of the pedigree dog, I suppose that I have always been aware that dogs appeared in a great number of paintings and that numerous examples have served as models for sculpture of all sorts. It was not, however, until I visited Madrid to judge dogs that I realised how important a part they played. Having visited galleries in almost all the major cities in the world, I had looked at paintings with the eye of an artist. But suddenly, in the Prado, I found that I was no longer looking at paintings as paintings, but that my eye was caught by dogs of all sorts, dogs of chase, running dogs and particularly companion dogs. The Prado has one of the best collections of works of art in the world and many of them, works by Velasquez, Murillo and Goya in particular, have as their subject family groups or members of a family surrounded by their favourite things, and especially dogs.

The mounting excitement of someone so interested in dogs surveying the walls of the Prado, and discovering dog after dog beautifully painted, is something that has to be experienced to be understood. Fortunately for us, the members of the royal and noble families of Spain were particularly attached to dogs, and frequently to toydogs. Many of the painters of the time who were commissioned to paint portraits of members of these families often included the dogs of the household in the idyllic surroundings in which they portrayed people. As it was the habit then to paint in a realistic manner, we have accurate records of many of the dogs of the time.

The Prado houses many fine paintings that are not Spanish, nor are they paintings of the Spanish scene or family, so that the walls are virtually a treasure-house of European history in picture form. The allegory on sight, for instance, painted by Jan Brueghel de Velours is a typical example. It is one of the early genre paintings of the interior of a collector's room and was painted in 1617.

Much of it is symbolic and many of the objects that appear round the walls of the room in the painting have been chosen to emphasise the allegory. Fortunately for us the artist has included a tiny toy spaniel confronting a monkey right in the foreground of the painting.

It is a spaniel, even though it apparently has a smooth coat. Its head is that of a spaniel and its ears are the typical pendant of the breed, but it is not like any toy spaniel that we know in its other details. Nevertheless the artist tells us a good deal about it. It is slightly timorous, looking out with an expression of guarded daring from beneath a footstool – prepared to challenge the monkey, but ready at the same time to retreat into its shelter should the monkey show signs of becoming too boisterous.

It is an interesting sidelight on the temperament of the different breeds, that even in those early days and in the same painting there is a small white woolly dog (it could be a bichon, or a Maltese terrier or even an example of the early shock dog), sitting quietly underneath the table nearby, watching what is going on but taking no part.

Artists have always been the recorders of their own times and even when, as in the case of the Jan Brueghel de Velours painting, they are involved in allegory and myth, the details of the scene in which the subject is set so often reveal a great deal about contemporary matters. So in this instance while the central theme of the painting is the semi-nude allegorical figure and the mythical winged faun, the dogs of the time, with not only their appearance clearly depicted but also their temperament.

Not only did the artists tell us something about those dogs that are still with us today, but also something about many that appear to have been lost to us. Tiziano, painting even earlier than de Velours, included a delightful dog in one of his portraits of the Prado which, if the animal existed today, would be one of the most glamorous of all toydogs – a long-haired Italian greyhound.

One of the most spectacular dogs in contemporary show rings is without doubt the saluki. Elegant, with the beautiful lines of the perfect machine, it has the added attraction of long flowing feathering which softens its outline when it is standing still and streams out like sunlit coloured liquids when it is running. Tiziano shows us just such a dog, but a miniature, something of the size of our present-day Italian greyhound but with all the glamour of the saluki – the long ear fringes, the feathering on the legs and the elegant neck of that breed. Attempts have been made from time to time to miniaturise some breeds, some have been successful, some not; but here we have an indication that at least one such dog existed in the middle of the sixteenth century.

The Italian greyhound, which is a very ancient breed and which was a favourite at court in both Spain and Italy centuries ago, appears frequently in paintings in the Prado. Surprisingly enough, in one case it appears with its ears cropped. Pugs certainly looked smart when they were cropped, but it was unusual to find this painting of the greyhound with its ear-lobes removed. It could well have been an exceptional case rather than common practice. It could even have been an error, like the docked Labradors I once saw, who were docked as puppies because the owner of the dam had feared a *mésalliance* with a boxer dog and had thought that boxer/Labradors would look better with short tails. However, the Italian greyhound looks strange, but no worse, with its ears shortened in the Prado painting. The cropping of the ears of pugs, mastiffs and some of the tougher breeds has always been accepted. The Neapolitan mastiff, for instance, has its ears cropped so short that they have almost disappeared, and will look odd with the long ears that it will have in the countries that are now importing the breed and where cropping is banned.

One of the most attractive paintings of an Italian greyhound proper must be the one that appears in the portrait 'The Earl of Northampton' by Pompeo Battoni in the Fitzwilliam Museum,

Cambridge. Perhaps a little large for its period – the mid-eighteenth century at which time the breed was really miniaturised – it still is a beautiful specimen, with all the elegance and grace of the breed, and painted in such accurate detail that it gives a more faithful impression of the breed than does many a present-day photograph.

Murillo's little white dog in 'The Holy Family of the Little Bird', painted in 1650, is one of the most delightful dog paintings in the Prado. This little white dog appears to have the face and eyes of a Maltese (the sort of solid white coat that none of our toy breeds at present have), and the tail of a Cavalier King Charles spaniel. It is not a bichon, the coat is not long enough, and although it has the ears of a King Charles spaniel it is white which makes that breed unlikely. It is almost certainly a breed that we have now lost or, and this is perhaps just as likely, it is a crossbred resulting from the inter-mixing of the various strains of tiny dogs that were the playthings of the houses of fashion and the courts of the mid-seventeenth century. Although the subject of Murillo's paintings is biblical, the artist often tended to include his own dogs in his paintings, the dogs that he saw around him, or even those belonging to the sponsors for whom he painted the picture. In this case the result is fascinating. The little dog sits in front of the Holy Family, clearly adoring the child, but at the same time it is doglike, with more than half an eye on the goldfinch which the child holds up in order to tempt him.

There are many more – Murillo's toy spaniels; similar little dogs in paintings by Maino; Ruben's toy spaniel complete with jewelled collar; paintings by Goya, Snyders, Boel and Velasquez, all well worth looking at. No description can do them justice, they can only be appreciated by standing in front of them and looking with the eye of both one who enjoys great art and one who appreciates dogs.

Many other galleries and private collections have paintings

Old print of King Charles spaniels showing clearly the white,
black and tan colouring which distinguished them from other
spaniels from 19th century engraving

that include toydogs. Few of them are just paintings of the dogs themselves, most being portraits with the dog or dogs included as one of the natural adjuncts of the person portrayed. There are exceptions to this, such as the portrait of the artist's dog 'Trump' by Hogarth, in the possession of the Kennel Club in London. Hogarth was not exceptional in that he owned dogs, or even toydogs, but few artists displayed their love of their pets as he did, including them, and particularly Trump, in a good many of his paintings and engravings. For example, in his engraving entitled 'Married to an Old Maid', Hogarth shows a very good, if long-legged, specimen of pug making up to what looks like a mini-boxer that sits on a stool.

Velasquez, in his painting 'Prince Phillip Prosper' in the Kunsthistorisches Museum, Vienna, painted a little dog very like the white toy spaniel in Murillo's 'Holy Family of the Little Bird'. Velasquez, however, portrays his dog completely at ease on a chair that it obviously considers its own. Velasquez painted the child in the rather formal manner of the time, staring out of the painting and paying no attention to the dog. The dog has one eye on the artist whilst appearing to be cocking an ear towards the child. One cannot escape the feeling that Velasquez painted the child because he was instructed to do so, while he painted the dog from sheer enjoyment.

Sir Joshua Reynolds (1723–92) painted dogs into his portraits at every opportunity, especially when he was painting children, which he often did. Frequently they were King Charles spaniels, as in his portrait of 'Maria Gideon and her Brother' in Viscount Cowdray's collection. In this painting the dog, a rather large and long-nosed version of the King Charles, has one paw raised, clearly ready for a game with the brother whom he obviously adores in spite of the fact that the boy is carrying a stick. It could be that he is waiting for the stick to be thrown.

In his painting of the family of George, 3rd Duke of Marl-borough, in the collection of the Duke of Marlborough, Reynolds again depicts Cavaliers. This time one is rather subdued, with its back towards the artist, but the other is determined to have a game with a somewhat reluctant black-and-white Italian greyhound. The Italian greyhound, looking a little timorous and in a typical pose with one paw raised, still manages to be very much one of the party.

Reynolds seems to have had a favourite dog although little is known about it. It looks something like a shih tzu, rather like a Maltese but coloured, and could well be a shock dog. It appears in his portrait of 'Princess Sophia Matilda of Gloucester' in the collection of Windsor Castle, as well as in those of 'Emelia Vansittart', Mrs Crewe, and in the portrait of Mrs Abington as Miss Prue in *Love for Love*. Most portrait painters worked under studio conditions, most of them still do, and it was the habit to have the studio well-equipped with lay figures, costumes, drapes and all sorts of accessories. The sitter only posed for fairly short periods of time whilst the actual physical details were painted. The rest of the painting – clothes, furniture, background and so on – were completed by the artist at his leisure without the model needing to be present. It rather appears that Reynolds had a pet dog as one of the accessories in his studio and he included the animal in a good many portraits. The dog must have led a great life, getting the attention of all the society beauties and children of its time.

Reynolds painted many other dogs too. In the portrait of Paul Cobb Methuen and Christian Methuen he depicts a cropped pug having a good chew after a flea, and in his portrait of 'Nellie O'Brien' there is what looks like an untrimmed toy poodle with its head comfortably on the lady's knee. It could of course have been a bichon, a breed once popular in France and now coming back to favour in the USA.

This type of dog, small, white and long-coated, appeared in a great number of paintings over the years. So many in fact that there is no doubt that it was a recognised breed. In the early seventeenth century Dirck Hals painted 'The Garden Party', now in the Rijksmuseum, in which there appears a tiny white dog looking very like a toy poodle with a curly tail. It sits in the foreground of an exotic landscape full of birds and mammals, which indicates that the owner of the estate kept something of a zoo. The dog in this case is being thoroughly entertained by a monkey which was another favourite animal for artists to include in this sort of work.

Later in the same century, around 1650, Adriaen van Ostade painted 'Interior with Skates', also in the Rijksmuseum. This could just as well have been called 'Interior with Shock Dog', as another little long-coated animal of the type, looking rather like a small white lowchen with the hindquarters clipped and with a tufted tail, appears just as prominently in the painting as do the skates that give the picture its name.

Other interesting toydogs appear in many paintings, having been included apparently at the whim of the artist. Many of them are strange to twentieth-century eyes. In the seventeenth century, Jacob Jordaens included what look like tiny white toy terriers in one of his paintings in the Royal Museum in Brussels. They have small domed skulls, tiny fold-back ears like a whippet and thin whippy tails like English toy terriers. They resemble rather fat white Manchester terriers and do not appear to be in the least interested in either Susanna or the Elders who form the main theme of the painting.

Earlier still, in the early sixteenth century, Frans Floris de Vrient painted a 'Holy Family' in which there appears a most interesting little dog looking like a Yorkshire terrier with flop ears. A tiny little dog, with a perfectly good Yorkie head, a long coat and a curly tail. It has the dark eyes, well-whiskered face and the shading of the Yorkshire terrier, and the only dog that I have seen like it in recent years was one that I photographed in South Africa,

which I believe was a cross between a Yorkshire terrier and a Chihuahua.

The inclusion of so many toydogs in paintings down the centuries emphasises the important part that they played in man's social life. In just the same way that painters have used the sports and pastimes of mankind, his architecture and interior decoration, and his parks and gardens as a setting for a sitter in order to establish what sort of man he was or what sort of family he had, so they have used his dogs to establish his personality. From allegory, right down to fairly recent paintings of either the genre type or the family portrait, the dog has played his part. Diana has had her greyhounds, Nastagio his fearsome hounds, and the families painted by Reynolds and Landseer their terriers and deerhounds.

The toydogs have, however, featured in paintings of all kinds from very early times. These paintings teach us not only that they were the regular companion of man and a very acceptable member of his household, but at the same time tell us a great deal about the dogs themselves. Nothing that is written can take the place of a visual representation, and those of us who are interested in dogs owe a great debt of gratitude to those painters who, by including dogs in their compositions, handed down to us a record of the appearance of toydogs through the centuries. How else would we have known that toy spaniels really did exist in the sixteenth century, or that there were once such things as long-haired Italian greyhounds and cropped-eared pugs? Life would be that little bit less rich if we could not walk round the Prado and the Rijksmuseum and see for ourselves.

Dogs were also from time to time included by artists just for fun, or so it appears, revealing the fact that even centuries ago these tiny dogs were thought to have appeal and the quality of irrepressibility. The little dog in 'Portrait of a Man and Woman' by Jacob Jordaens in the National Gallery, London, is a typical example. There was no apparent reason for the inclusion of this

little dog, apart from those of composition, or at least so it appears. It may well have belonged to the couple depicted, but although it has been included by the artist it is not involved with the sitters. It sits at the man's feet, looking out of the painting, and it is the most delightful and comic little character. Something like Maltese, something like a lowchen, it could well have been yet another bichon frise. What it does tell us is that in the early part of the seventeenth century there was a little toydog that at least one portrait painter found irresistible.

There is a similar example in 'Hermes, Herse and Aglauros' by Veronese in the Fitzwilliam Museum in Cambridge, a toy spaniel this time, dating from the middle of the sixteenth century when they were just known as toy spaniels and had not become separated into individual breeds. Again, the dog is not included as an essential part of the group, nor apparently with any idea of family association. It just seized the imagination of the painter because he found it fascinating. Once more it is a cocky little dog looking for mischief, and apparently having recently finished playing with, of all things, a rose, which has now been abandoned.

The little toydog included in 'The Broken Mirror' by Greuze, painted in about the middle of the eighteenth century, is interesting to us for another reason. Once more it has been included by the artist as part of the setting, in this case showing keen interest in the mirror that lies shattered on the floor. But the real point, from the view of both one dog-fancier and the artist, is that it closely resembles the dog used by Kirchner for his Meissen porcelain called 'The Bolognese Hound'. It has the same colouration and the same spiky look about the hair.

Nicholas de Largillière included a papillon, or rather a phalene, in his painting of 'Louis XIV and his heirs' in the early eighteenth century, again not just because it happened to be there, but clearly because he found it fascinating. Fortunately for us he could paint dogs, and although the 'Bolognese' of Greuze is a most unlikely shape this phalene is beautifully depicted in virtually the same position. Again, one has the feeling that this particular little dog was included by the artist for sheer pleasure. He was under commission to paint people, and it shows. The resulting contrast between the pompous and somewhat supercilious people and the self-assertive little dog conveys a good deal to the student of human nature. It has been claimed that there are other reasons for including dogs in paintings. A story has grown up around 'Arnolfini's marriage', for instance, that the fluffy little dog in the painting signifies wedded bliss and domestic harmony. Perhaps there's a moral in this somewhere?

Dogs, and toydogs in particular, have been a favourite subject for the craftsman in porcelain and earthenware. The toydogs, being smaller in size, were somehow more appropriate for this type of work, but it is true that other and larger dogs have from time to time been used. The greyhound, for instance, has for centuries been traditionally depicted by the Staffordshire potters with or without a dead hare and with or without a tree stump to lean against – the latter not because it was weary, but simply that for technical reasons such a thin-legged animal needs some support.

In Chinese work it is sometimes difficult to distinguish between the lion and the dog. In fact there is some doubt as to whether they can be distinguished at all, the lion-dog and the dog-lion having shared Chinese myth until they are more or less synonymous. However, there is no doubt that the dogs of Fo of the reign of K'ang Hsi were indeed dogs. The Emperor K'ang Hsi set up an imperial kiln in the city of Peking in 1680. In this city at that time it was possible that there were a million people working in porcelain at 3,000 kilns, a production situation such as no other country has ever matched.

(*facing page*) Italian greyhounds at play from an engraving by Reinagle 1820

Pottery pug Staffordshire 19th century

Dogs of Fo, sometimes confusingly called guardian lions, are encountered quite frequently, generally in pairs and usually with the male playing with the traditional woven ball and the female with one of her cubs. They were made in huge quantities between 1662 and 1722. They were undoubtedly small dogs of the Pekingese type, and although they had something of a lionlike look so has the Pekingese, and as lions were hardly familiar objects in China there is much more likelihood that they were indeed little dogs.

Pugs in pottery are depicted with much more frequency. Kaendler, who modelled at the Meissen factory, used them often. They were then, in about 1750, called Möpser, a name still in use for pugs in Europe. Probably because of their quaint appearance and the fact that as they are solid little dogs they lent themselves to being reproduced by casting in a mould, they were a favourite subject. The ones that were produced in 1740 were in fact called hounds, but they were very little like the accepted idea of a hound and were undoubtedly pugs with closely cropped ears. A good deal of artistic licence was allowed to the modellers and designers, and the Meissen hounds of that period came in colours and patterns that would be looked at askance by breeders and exhibitors of pugs of today.

The eighteenth-century Staffordshire potters who had up to that time been subsisting on the production of a great quantity of fairly crude 'peasant pottery', decided that if they were to survive they must produce something much more professional looking. They began to produce models of pugs. Their early efforts, such as those of John Dwight, were still somewhat crude and fairly grotesque representations of the dogs. Although these pieces of pottery are becoming increasingly valuable, they are not the sort of thing that the expert of today would accept as typical of the breed. These eighteenth-century pugs are pot-bellied, long in the leg and have the most peculiar expression.

The model of Hogarth's Trump, now attributed to Louis François Roubiliac (1702/5–62) the French sculptor who worked in England from 1732, was a great step forward. There is still some doubt as to which of the factories produced the finished articles, it could have been Chelsea or it could have been one of the other factories then currently in production, but whichever it was resulted in something very much more like a dog that the early Staffordshire efforts. At least the head is that of a pug, and although its tail is suspect and its legs rather long, it could well be that the original was in fact built that way.

Pugs are still produced today. They look more like the breed all the time, but unfortunately they don't improve as pieces of pottery *per se*. Technically it is easier to make casts from moulds when the moulds themselves are less complicated and smoother, so that as time went by the wrinkles and details tended to disappear, and with them the character of the dog. Mass-production too is fairly destructive, and much of the latter pottery produced lacked character as pottery as well as losing a good deal of the character of the dog.

One of the most interesting little dogs portrayed in porcelain was the dog of Madame de Pompadour, produced in Vincennes around 1750. This was almost certainly a Maltese, its coat, fringes and tail as well as the details of the head being definitely those of this breed. Antoinette Poisson was of humble birth, but rapidly acquired good taste when she became marquise and persuaded Louis XV to support the Vincennes factory. The little Maltese, now a rare collector's piece, is reputed to be the marquise's own dog and was probably modelled in the factory as a tribute to her interest.

The so-called Bolognese hound, an example of which is in the Museum of Art, New York, is fascinating to those interested in dogs. There is no hound breed that looks anything like the dog depicted, but there is at least one toydog that does. The model looks very like a furious Maltese with long coat and terrier-type head. The original was produced by Johann Gottlieb Kirchner for the Meissen factory as part of a collection to furnish the Japanese palace of Augustus the Strong, and the oriental influence is very marked in the model. If the spiky hair around the head and ears and the near-foliated oriental tail is ignored, the resultant dog could well be a long-eared short-haired Maltese showing more anger than the average dog of this breed. (John P. Cushion, in his book *Animals in Pottery and Porcelain* refers to an old description of the Bolognese as another 'ladies' dog, portrayed as somewhat sad and plaintive in nature due to the 'hound's' large dark eyes which seem always to be tearful. It then goes on to describe a small white dog with long silk coat and pendant ears and a tail carried over the back, mingling its hair with the body coat. All of this seems to fit the Maltese so aptly that I subscribe to the view that the Bolognese portrayed by Kirchner was in fact a Maltese, and I would go so far as to suggest that all so-called Bolognese were in fact Maltese that had found their way to Bologna.)

Another breed of toydog that has been a real favourite of the pottery modeller over the centuries has been the toy spaniel. At one time few households were without representations of their pet dog, or even a pair of pot dogs, sitting on the mantelpiece in the front parlour. These were invariably toy spaniels and almost certainly Cavalier King Charles spaniels, some of them having the tell-tale spot of colour on the skull. Technically the production of pottery figures, particularly in earthenware, is simplified if the mould can be made in just two parts, the clay pressed in to each half by hand and then the two halves joined together. The reason for the traditional shape of the King Charles spaniel pot dogs is that they are made thus in two halves, the one half containing the back of the sitting dog and the other half the front with the feet and head. If the model is examined carefully the join can usually be found even in the best finished of them.

In spite of the fact that they were turned out in their thousands

Typical head of a Staffordshire pottery spaniel, 1820–50 possession of the author

these models have great charm, the details of the face being painted on by hand, and each one being slightly different from the next. Most of the colour work on them was executed by young people, and somehow there is an air of enjoyment about the way in which the detail is painted on, which is not only youthful but which also has something in keeping with the whole character of toydogs. Toydogs have a quaintness and an appeal which somehow transmits itself to people, and particularly young people, and the girls (which they often were) who painted the features on pottery spaniels seemed to do so with a certain flair and sympathy even though the work must have been totally repetitive.

The age in which these models were produced was that of the English sportsman, a time when gundogs and hounds were not just status symbols but accepted as the types of dog that were appropriate. The big estates had their gundogs and the working man had his running dogs, and anything less than a hound or a gundog was despised to a degree.

Yet the dog which became immensely popular as a decoration at that time was the antithesis of the sporting dog. Said to have been a cross between a Maltese and a King Charles spaniel, the result was popularly known as a 'comforter' or 'spaniel's gentle', a lady's dog, a lap warmer and a finicky little creature of the boudoir. As such it was undoubtedly scorned to a certain extent, even by those who were producing and painting them as pot dogs. The result was that even when earthenware dogs had achieved a standard of technical excellence that was a remarkable transition from the early Staffordshire primitives, they still retained a quaintness that gave them a certain charm. This charm has lasted through the years until now in the twentieth century the pot dog has re-emerged as one of the more popular artifacts used for interior decoration.

The typical specimen dates from around 1820–50, the less-romantic period of Staffordshire ware, and their naïveté retains something of the earlier work superimposed on the superior technique of the later periods. The majority were sold at country fairs and for fairings, for that is virtually what they were, and they were of a surprisingly high quality. By early Victorian times hardly a cottage was without its pottery figures and the dog, that featured so large in the life of country people, was a natural choice to become a popular subject. Bow, Worcester and Chelsea all produced dogs, but it was the Staffordshire potteries that turned them out in their thousands.

Almost every breed was modelled at some time or another, and no two are ever absolutely identical. The expression and the colour pattern differs from potter to potter and from painter to painter, so that although they all looked alike they were each in a subtle way slightly different from the next. This is part of their appeal. These little spaniels, or 'comforters' as they were known, were always made in pairs, the natural love of symmetry at the time dictating that they should face one another from opposite ends of the mantelpiece. They were almost always white, with spots and patches of red or gold on ears and body. A common feature is the padlock hanging from the collar and a chain slung across the brisket and over the back, often in gold.

These models do not tell us much about the breed of dog of the time as they are so formal and standardised in style and type but they do tell us that dogs, and particularly toydogs, enjoyed a tremendous popularity in the early nineteenth century. The Möps, the German version of the pug, was also fairly popular as a pottery figure. It is often depicted with its toes turned up, its tongue out and its head toward the right. If the Möps had a finely painted insect on each side of its neck, this was intended as a symbol of fidelity and is associated with the Society of Mopses, a Roman Catholic organisation.

In the nineteenth century white pugs with curled tails were produced at the Bow pottery. One of the potteries which also

Early black Pomeranian from Vero Shaw's Book of The Dog 1881

produced a number of models of dogs was the Rockingham works, a pottery with a fascinating history in which the Fitzwilliam family were at one time involved. They produced miniatures of lapdogs and poodles, but they also made models of toy spaniels seated on cushions. Between 1820 and 1840 they were making models of poodles which involved a complicated and attractive technique in which the hair was produced by clay extrusion. These have now become very much collectors' pieces and are quite valuable.

Toydogs have never been favourites with artists and craftsmen working in materials other than clay. There have been some fine pieces of work produced in bronze, particularly by French artists and sculptors, but they have been largely of sporting dogs, hounds and gundogs. The Chinese craftsmen, however, produced examples of their lion dog in almost every medium from porcelain to ivory, but as there is still a good deal of confusion about the identity of the animal it is difficult to make a claim that a tiny dog carved as a netsuke, for instance, is a Pekingese when it could well be something quite different.

Some marble carvers produced fine and accurate pieces of sculpture of dogs. For example, the author owns a beautiful marble by Gott of a boy with a family of Italian greyhounds. In common with all such work, the details of the dogs is extremely accurate and it is possible to tell just what this particular bitch and her roly-poly looked like a hundred years ago.

Works of art depicting dogs, whether they be paintings, sculpture or one of the decorative crafts, serve a twofold purpose. They teach us a good deal about the dogs of the past as there is no doubt that the eye of the artist is a trained eye – in fact one wonders if all dog judges should not have a course in art appreciation. In this way, paintings take the place of the camera which records the dogs of today for posterity. In addition they have their own intrinsic merits as works of art.

Canaletto painted the buildings and the canals of Venice, Constable the trees and churches of East Anglia, and Van Gogh his chairs and sunflowers. The buildings of Venice, the trees and churches, and chairs and sunflowers have changed very little, and each in its turn served as the subject-matter for great works of art. Hogarth, Landseer and Stubbs did much the same with dogs, each in his turn using their form, colour and character to create works of art.

Unfortunately there is no one today to carry on the great tradition of animal painting. There *are* animal painters, but most of them are concerned with portraying pedigree dogs because they make a living out of doing so – few if any are painting animals, and dogs in particular, for sheer pleasure. Many of our major painters, concerned as they are with the abstract, the expressionistic or the surreal, do not find the dog attractive material, which may be just as well as the results if they did may be rather horrifying to the average owner of the pedigree dog. If the pendulum swings back, and our artists begin again to consider the possibilities of realism and naturalism, perhaps once more some of them will rediscover the dog as suitable material.

Cavalier King Charles spaniel

INDEX